GW00361431

HISTRIONIC/

HIƧTRIONICƧ
Three Plays

Thomas Bernhard

Translated by
Peter Jansen *and* Kenneth Northcott

The University of Chicago Press • Chicago and London

THOMAS BERNHARD (1931–89) was a playwright, poet, and
novelist whose prestigious literary prizes include the Austrian
State Prize, the Büchner Prize, the Bremen Prize, and Le Prix
Séguier. His novels *Woodcutters, Concrete, Gargoyles,* and *The
Lime Works* are also available in English translation from the
University of Chicago Press. KENNETH NORTHCOTT is
professor emeritus in the Department of Germanic Languages
and Literatures at the University of Chicago. PETER K. JANSEN
is associate professor of German at the University of Chicago.

The three plays in this volume were originally published in three
separate volumes as *Ein Fest für Boris* (© 1968), *Ritter, Dene, Voss*
(© 1984), and *Der Theatermacher* (© 1984) by Suhrkamp Verlag,
Frankfurt am Main.

The University of Chicago Press, Chicago 60637
© 1990 by The University of Chicago
All rights reserved. Published 1990
Printed in the United States of America

99 98 97 96 95 94 93 92 91 90   5 4 3 2 1

Library of Congress Cataloging-in-Publication Data

Bernhard, Thomas.
  [Plays. English. Selections]
  Histrionics: Three plays / Thomas Bernhard; translated by
Peter Jansen and Kenneth Northcott.
    p. cm.
  Contents: A party for Boris—Ritter, Dene, Voss—
Histrionics.
  ISBN 0–226–04394–0 (alk. paper). — ISBN 0–226–04395–9
(pbk.: alk. paper)
  1. Bernhard, Thomas—Translations, English. I. Title.
PT2662.E7A25 1990
832'.914—dc20   89–20198
                                                     CIP

⊗ The paper used in this publication meets the minimum
requirements of the American National Standard for Information
Sciences—Permanence of Paper for Printed Library Materials,
ANSI Z39.48–1984.

CONTENTS

BIOGRAPHICAL NOTE

Thomas Bernhard was born in Heerlen, Holland, to an Austrian mother, on February 9th (or 10th), 1931. His mother was the daughter of Johannes Freumbichler, an author of regional renown. The boy spent his early years under the tutelage of his mother's parents, in Vienna and in the country. After a year at boarding school, he worked for a few months as a gardener in the small town of Traunstein and was subsequently enrolled at the Salzburg Johanneum, a Catholic school. In 1947 he dropped out of school to become apprenticed to a local grocer. An attack of pleurisy in 1948 marked the beginning of a series of pulmonary disorders that caused his confinement in a sanitarium until 1951. It was while there, at Grafendorf, that he began to compose poetry. In 1952 he enrolled at the Salzburg Mozarteum Academy to study music and theatre, graduating in 1957 with a thesis on Artaud and Brecht. While attending the Mozarteum, Bernhard also worked as a court reporter for the *Demokratische Volksblatt*, a Salzburg socialist newspaper. From 1957 on Bernhard was a freelance writer. He worked and lived in Poland and England. In 1965 he made his home on a farm in Ohlsdorf, Upper Austria, where he resided until his death in 1989.

Bernhard's writing develops chronologically from verse to prose (both fiction and autobiography) and to drama. His first play, *A Party for Boris*, was produced in 1968. Altogether Bernhard was the author of some forty-five works of literature and was, in the last two decades, the most prolific writer for the German-speaking stage. Of the forty-five works, the following are currently listed in *Books in Print* as being available in translation: *Concrete*, Knopf and University of Chicago; *Correction*, Random; *Gargoyles*, University of Chicago; *Gathering Evidence*, Knopf; *The Lime Works*, University of Chicago; *The President and Eve of Retirement,* PAJ Publications (this contains a very useful introductory essay by Gitta Honegger); and *Woodcutters,* Knopf.

Among the numerous awards Bernhard received, two deserve special mention, namely, the Austrian State Prize for Literature (1967) and the Georg Büchner Prize (1970).

TRANSLATORS' NOTE

Thomas Bernhard does not use punctuation—except on one occasion—and we have, of course, done our translation with this in mind. He does use capital letters at certain points—generally to indicate a change of thought or, possibly, a pause. However, those readers who are familiar with the German language will realize that all nouns are printed with a capital letter at the beginning, so that when a line begins with a noun, ambiguities are bound to arise. We have used our own judgment in these cases.

We should also point out that Bernhard's style is characterized on many occasions by disjunctions in his use of language and that these disjunctions are often represented by unusual or previously nonexistent constructions in German. Where these occur in the English text, it is important that the actor or the director be aware of this fact and not assume that there is some infelicity in the translation. Great care has been taken over these passages, as they form an integral part of the play.

A WORD ABOUT *A PARTY FOR BORIS*

A Party for Boris is the first play Thomas Bernhard wrote. In spite of the obvious difficulties of staging, the work has been performed successfully both in Germany and Austria. After the first performance of the play in Munich, the critic of *Die Zeit*, one of Germany's very influential newspapers, especially in the cultural field, said: "In any case no one could go home thinking of an idiotically ceremonious global metaphor (for example, 'we are all cripples, our world is a global asylum') but with this play about cripples, the sickness of Munich theatrical life has finally been cured."

While it is certainly not our intention to suggest ways in which the play should be staged, we would urge that full rein be given to the rich vein of humor that runs through this and all of Bernhard's plays. It is the contrast between this humor and the extremity of the situation that gives the play its extraordinary power. Perhaps too—before the play is subjected to an agonizing, and probably fruitless, analysis—it is important to recall the words of the critic of the *Salzburger Nachrichten:* "What is the point of the whole thing? The question is irrelevant. Bernhard creates a vision, draws dark calligrams, forms extreme situations and attitudes, demarcates the line between wakefulness and dream, between sadism and masochism, insanity and over-clever systematization, offers linguistic elements which permit the words to sparkle with a multiplicity of meaning when they are repeated: in a word he is a sort of magician."

A PARTY FOR BORIS

"Admittedly, first nights are usually intolerable examinations
and a mockery of art."
   —Aleksandr Blok

In the Good Woman's House

Dramatis Personae
The Good Woman, *legless*
Johanna
Boris, *legless*
Thirteen legless cripples from the home for cripples
Two servants
Two attendants
All the legless in wheelchairs

First Prologue

Empty room, high windows and doors
The Good Woman *right*
Johanna *enters from left with a table and places it by The Good Woman*
The Good Woman
　　It's cold
Johanna *moves the table still closer to The Good Woman and places herself behind her*
The Good Woman
　　Heavens it's cold
　　Bring me the blanket
Johanna *hesitates*
The Good Woman *roughly*
　　Bring me the blanket
　　I'm freezing
　　because I've been sitting here for a whole hour
　　and haven't moved
Johanna *makes to go*
The Good Woman
　　Wait
　　wait
　　Have you mailed the letters
　　the letters the letter to the home

to the mayor
to the police chief
realizes that she has not posted them
    All right then tear them up
    throw them away
Johanna *makes to leave*
The Good Woman
    No bring them here
Johanna
    All of them
The Good Woman
    All of them
    Today the envelopes are green
    and tomorrow they'll be white again
    and so on
    You've been laughing about this for over three years
    If only you could laugh my illness away
    But hurry up and bring me the letters
    so that I can tear them all up
    Every day everything is everyday
    a repetition of repetitions
    All night long and all morning
    I've been writing letters again
    Untruths
    inadequacies
    lies
    lies about lies
    Why do I lie
    All these lies are obfuscations
    that everything is true and actual
shrieking
    For Heaven's sake why don't you forbid me
    to write letters
    If only suddenly
    quite suddenly
    I weren't to know any more addresses
    knew nothing of those addresses
    not a single address
    If every name were suddenly wiped from my memory
    every single name
    If I were no longer to know
    what associations these names and addresses had
    It's killing me

it's killing me Johanna
But every night I write those letters
exit **Johanna**
The Good Woman
One great big lie
everything
shrieking after her
Don't you dare let me write any more letters
Why don't you take the stationery away from me for heaven's sake
Go on take it away from me
When you see me start
to write letters
see that it's madness
untruths
lies
I order you not to let me
write any more letters
to herself
I want to go to sleep
and I can't go to sleep
and I keep pondering
out loud again
And then I order you
to bring me the stationery
and you bring me the stationery
to herself
I must do something
if I do nothing
nothing
horrible
Johanna *enters with the letters*
The Good Woman
Give them to me
hides the letters in the drawer of the table
Later
later
But why aren't there any newspapers today
Johanna
They're on strike
The Good Woman
Who's on strike
Johanna
The printers

The Good Woman
  The printers
Johanna
  They're all on strike
The Good Woman
  They're all on strike
  Suddenly they're all on strike
  Everybody's on strike
  Everybody
Johanna
  They're on strike everywhere
The Good Woman
  Everybody's on strike
  This strike will also have an effect on us
  If it goes on for a long time
  Are there enough vegetables in the house
  fruit
  meat
  If the strike goes on for a time
  Everything points to the strike
  going on for quite a time
  No newspapers
  that's horrible
  The advertisements
  The murders
  and the weather
  Apart from books
  there are no diversions left for me anymore
  Do bring me the blanket
exit **Johanna**
The Good Woman *brooding*
  Read read
out loud
  By the way yesterday you gave me
  another play in which a man appears
  who no longer has legs
  recently you seem to have taken a delight in giving me the sort of
                                                      literature

  in which cripples play a part
  sadistic
  but I forgive you
  we forgive each other
  After all you aren't
  really ill-intentioned

you're ill-natured
not ill-intentioned
that little difference after the first syllable
makes it possible for me to keep on putting up with you
Forbid me ever to write a single letter again
You must promise me to do that

Johanna *enters with a blanket and wraps* **The Good Woman** *in it*
The Good Woman
    I can't get to sleep
    and I read those novels those plays
suddenly out loud
    For heaven's sake open the windows
    I'm suffocating
Johanna *opens the windows*
The Good Woman
    You have to make it impossible for me
    impossible
    If I don't mail the letters
    it doesn't matter
softly
    You must stop it
    prevent me from doing it
    The truth is that no one wants to get a letter from me
    no one
    nothing
    because I'm stuck in one single spot
    Then then
    lots of things occur to me of course
    so much occurs to me that I am afraid
    that my ideas could be fatal
    my ideas
    No one has time for letters
    For ideas
    it is true that people have no ideas
    because they have no time
    for ideas
    and they have no time
    because they have no ideas
    nobody likes to live like a specter
    I have the most time
    and I have no time at all
    that is my misfortune
    My ideas bore me
    If I were suddenly to have no more ideas

My immobility Johanna
If I tell you to tear up my letters
you go out and you read them
and only after you have read them
do you throw them away
Tear them up
And if I say you may not read them
before throwing them away
you read them
I have always thrown my letters away torn up
in all the ten years that my husband has been dead
I have torn up all my letters again and again
it's true
I haven't mailed a single letter
That's true admit it
Torn up
burnt
There's no reason at all to upset me like this Johanna
Why *do* I upset myself
to a letter which is not mailed
no answer can
No no Johanna
With the questions the answers and so on
Johanna you presume to know everything about me
because you've been in my house for three years
because you've been here three years
before that you did not exist
You're full of presumption

exit **Johanna**

The Good Woman
She's aware of everything
she knows everything
she knows what's in my chest of drawers

out loud after her
Of course you know that
You're right
You've been in my house for three years

Johanna *enters with a huge white cardboard box*

The Good Woman
What's that you've got

Johanna
The gloves the hats

The Good Woman
The gloves the hats

Johanna *places the box on the table*
The Good Woman
   The gloves the hats
From now until the curtain falls she keeps trying on long gloves, which
   reach at least to her elbows, red, green, yellow, but above all
   white and black ones, and large spring hats in the same colors
   while **Johanna** *helps her*
The Good Woman
   Did you tell the glover
   that I shall choose only one single pair
   that I cannot decide immediately
   One pair of gloves
   One hat
   Of course you know
   what I have
   You know what I own
   as I sit here
   in my armchair
   everything
   you are aware of everything
   If only you knew all the things there are
   of which you are not aware
bursts into laughter
   My bad taste
   which is a result of my good taste
   Because you are an intelligent person
   And because you are so intelligent
   you often keep your mouth shut
   It is misuse
   everything is misuse
   In an intelligent way your reticence
   the reticence of your intelligence
   Your intelligence to pronounce a long and witty sentence
   without a single error
   to pronounce without a single error
   a long witty sentence
   which is related to French for example
   although you don't understand this sentence at all
   and although you have never once
   heard this sentence before
   never read it or heard it
   You pronounce foreign names
   most intelligently
   French adverbs for example

You read aloud excellently
you can pronounce the most difficult sentences
without a single error
For ten years the most important thing for me has been
to have someone who could read aloud excellently
Your predecessor
No
a woman who can pronounce the most difficult sentences
without a single error
you do pronounce French names excellently
for example the word *oublié*
The way you pronounce that
not too fast
Don't you see that the glove is too small for me
they're all too small for me
throws a pair on to the floor
Johanna *picks them up*
The Good Woman
The others the others
throwing a glove in her face
It's not my fault
it's dreadful having to listen
to a sentence completely mispronounced
if only you knew how that pains me
Those are *my* pains Johanna
How old are you
tell me how old
you are
You won't tell me because
I ask you every day how old you are
But I want to know how old you are
No I'll spare you that
You don't need to tell me how old you are
Not today
Not now
The white one the white one
Johanna *puts a white glove on* **The Good Woman's** *hand and places a*
white hat on her head
The Good Woman
I have noticed over and over again that people
who haven't the faintest idea
of what they are reading aloud
read what they read excellently

There was one time when you already knew a chapter
do you remember
You know the chapter I mean
You can remember exactly
You had read it to yourself without permission
before you read it aloud to me
and it was unbearable
to listen to you
Do you remember
we had to break off the reading
break off
We broke off the reading
Watch out you're breaking my fingers
I remember how you read me
the article about my visit to the orphans
and to the municipal schools for retarded children
with unbelievable aplomb
You have an astonishing appreciation
of criminal journalistic sentence structures
Do you remember
all the time I think
about what it is that plays so great a part
in our relationship
When I see you
when I only as much as hear you
I only need to hear you
I only need to think about you
and there it is
When I only so much as think about you
Why do I mistrust you
You've been in my house for three full years
and I mistrust you
mistrust your very thought processes
The first time I saw you
the mistrust was there
putting on a green hat and green gloves
A rainy day
a terrible rainy day
do you remember that it was a rainy day
You repelled me
The truth is that from the very first moment
You repelled me
You infected me with your illness

We are joined to each other in a relationship of sickness
the whole world consists of such sicknesses
all of which have gone undiagnosed
laughing
I told you to change your clothes
change
stay
You became one of my possessions
Change your clothes and stay
I said
and you changed your clothes and did stay
Your voice
Your sense of nuance
tearing the gloves from her hands and the hat from her head and
throwing everything onto the floor
of those preposterous associations
Above all the way you drew the curtains
repelled me
The way you opened the curtains
looking at the floor
For heaven's sake pick them up
Why on earth don't you pick them up
Johanna *picks up the hat and the gloves*
The Good Woman, *after* **Johanna** *has picked up the hat and the gloves*
throws everything as far away as possible
Bring me everything
Johanna *fetches hat and gloves*
The Good Woman
Now you draw the curtains differently
not so abruptly any more
That would make no difference
On the very first day
you became entangled in contradictions
that immediately
interested me
You said that as a five-year-old child
you had lost your parents
It was a lie
Your father was tall
you described him as short
You grew up in a cramped room
Your mother could sing
only you didn't hear it
You had a relationship with a dog

only you didn't realize it
The green ones
the green ones
trying on green gloves, putting on a green hat
During the whole of the first year
you didn't say a word about my late husband
as if you had sensed that for the whole first year
you were not allowed to talk about my late husband
Your sensibility
Your absolute feeling
for the sublime
Johanna
You did sense it
but after a year you suddenly asked me
and I can even still remember where
there in front of that window
this situation
We were talking about the conditions
which prevail in the home
and that I was thinking of
taking one of those wretched cripples from the home
into my own house
of marrying such a cripple
Then you asked me whether my husband
had said anything before he died
No nothing
You kept on asking me whether my husband
had said anything before he died
Your brutal frankness
In your morbid way
you wanted to find out details
My husband was killed instantly
I was not killed
But my husband was killed instantly
my legs were gone
You keep wanting to hear something connected with the accident
connected with that evening
No matter what you asked me
When you ask me about my nightgown
about my necklace
When you ask me whether I want to go out or go downstairs
then you're really only asking
what the accident was like
That rainy day

I knew you were the right person for me
A cripple I said
a cripple who like me
has no legs any longer
bring him home
marry him
Boris
The whole process reminds me of that afternoon
when I bought myself the dog
The very moment when I knew
that I owned you
I didn't want the dog any longer
You took the dog away yourself
You remember don't you that you took the dog away
took it out
took it downstairs
You hated that dog
You were happy that the dog was no longer there
Johanna *starts to say something*
The Good Woman
Be quiet
You hated that dog from the first moment
You discovered that dog
You discovered yourself
and hated it
and hated yourself
You hated the poor animal
You couldn't have endured having to compete with that dog
It wasn't hard for me to part with the dog
It couldn't jump up on me any more
it was old
I held it here
see here
here on my lap
The dog didn't cause me half the trouble
The dog's already on the leash but you
It took a year in your case
but because I knew
it would be difficult
because you are so complicated
Your predecessors
No
Not one of them as complicated as you
The problem was and is

that you don't come from the country
Your predecessors came from the country
that makes things simpler
It was clear to me from the first moment that with you
it would not be so easy
You resisted
You hated me
You hate me now
At that time you hated me without knowing
why you hated me
You did not expect this job to be the way it is
easier
You expected everything would be easier
Expectations
false expectations
This house and I
But your complications
are not as difficult as my complications
You are exceptionally intelligent
and senseless
When two people make a mutual habit of each other
and
although they despair
of making an art out of that habit
I can see you still in your insipid stockings
those insipid shoes you were wearing
that rainy day
We have both made a habit of each other
Once you start putting up with that
Habit
hypocrisy
My habit if it is a habit
Everything is a misunderstanding when it comes to servants
At first you resisted
You wanted to break out
leave
Your attempts at breaking out
I can remember every attempt you made to break out
You didn't leave
throwing a glove in Johanna's face
In fear you were in fear
and that fear of yours
your fear and mine then grew into
this dreadful permanent state

You asked for more and more money
I gave you more and more money
but in the end had to spoil
everything again with your feelings
In those days you read me one after the other
all those famous nineteenth-century Russian novels
You remember
Oblomov
Dolgoruky
Crazy
A cripple defeated you
defeated us
a cripple
Boris
Of course I had to pay a high price
for our relationship
Then I set the trap for you
I threatened you
You threatened me
We hardly exist any more except in threats
With every threat from my side our relationship is
with every threat from your side
give it to me
give it
putting on a black hat
Magnificent
Black gloves
Johanna *gives The Good Woman black gloves*
The Good Woman
It reminds me of the funeral
*taking the black gloves off again, throwing them away, taking off the
black hat and throwing it away*
Not black
Black no
Johanna *picks up hat and gloves*
The Good Woman
It really galls me
You would have remained what you were
the totally common person
that you were
When I think what your circumstances would have made of you
You must admit
that you wouldn't have liked it

your life
You wouldn't have liked that common life of yours
You are more intelligent than you want me to know
You only show me your superficial intelligence
You show me the intelligence which I observe
when you fetch me a glass of water
pick up my hat
when you wash the stumps of my legs
when you dress me
undress me
comb my hair
How very intelligent you are when you comb me
no one has ever combed me with such great intelligence
You have the sort of intelligence
that has interested me all my life
Oh those gloves
give them to me
putting on the black gloves once again, putting on the black hat once
again
It's true that you would never have escaped
from your commonness
You have no eye
for human misery
for the misery of humanity
There is a difference between one kind of hatred
and another
Do you still remember
how I used to send you every day day after day
for a pair of stockings
and each time to a different shop
But you don't know anything about Lord Byron either
Every day I sent you out for a pair of stockings
although I no longer have legs
and although you knew perfectly well that I have no legs any more
you ran off to get the stockings
each and every day
to a different shop
do you remember the shoemaker
who I had measure me for a pair of shoes
and who measured me for them
although he knew
that I had no legs and therefore no feet any longer
he measured me for the shoes

do you remember
taking off the black gloves, taking the black hat off her head and
    dropping everything
That man
that unbelievably skillful man
those beautiful shoes
which I have so often
let you borrow
over and over again
Your intelligence rests on the fact
that you have seen a lot in my company
There are highly intelligent people who see nothing
see and that makes them unhappy
give me the red ones the red ones
putting on red gloves and a red hat
You're hurting me
laughing
The masses see nothing
the masses are not unhappy either
the masses are happy
At this point I have always asked you
what time it is
with her arms stretched out wide
Every day in these three years
at three o'clock sharp I have always asked you
what time it is
and you have always answered me
Three o'clock
If only once you had not answered me
if only on one single occasion you had not answered me
It's a game
taking the gloves off, throwing the hat away, **Johanna** *picks everything*
    up
It is the darkness
And the brooding
And the idleness
Because you constantly leave me on my own
when I talk
You stand there the whole time and only move
when I order you to move
I am convinced that immobility
that fatal illness
in nature
every disease is a disease

of immobility
You don't move
You see
You brood
You see me drop down dead
You see me dead in my chair dead
It's always the same you see me dead
dead
You wait
for me to be dead
A dead woman
You always see it
holding up a pair of yellow gloves laughing
It's those crazy notions
that's all
How far have I traveled
where have they all traveled to
we always traveled all of us traveled traveled
throwing the gloves away, **Johanna** *picks them up*
Don't you ever feel the need to travel
far away simply to travel far
we traveled everywhere
trying on a green glove
But if you travel to England
and do not understand the English language
or to Russia and don't understand any Russian
It's a good thing
that I put a stop to it
a stop
very softly
a stop
admiring the green glove
It wasn't as if I had been surprised by the accident
that's not how it was
taking the green glove off again
To be dead
to plunge into a light shaft
to be dead like my husband
To tell the truth it's been weeks since I last dreamed about him
Years
When you shine your shoes
don't you think about me
when you cross your legs
You feel comfortable in the thought

which isn't a thought
You think I'll go upstairs
or I'll go downstairs
go out
go away
because I have legs that's what you think
You have legs
When you keep running around the house
Recently you've spent so much time running around
You run around all morning long
all afternoon
when you go to meet your boyfriend
don't you think about me then
a person is a person
who has fallen in hate with another person
When is the party
Johanna when is the party
When *are* they coming
When

Johanna
Tuesday

The Good Woman
Tuesday
Tuesday Boris's birthday
And when is the ball

Johanna
Tomorrow

The Good Woman
Tuesday the party
Tomorrow the ball
Tuesday the party
Oh the conditions in that home
That person
To tell the truth the only thing I've been interested in all my life
is the relationship between two human beings
What's the time
No don't tell me what the time is

Johanna *puts a pair of red gloves on* **The Good Woman** *and puts a red
   hat on her head*

The Good Woman
Twenty-five past three
admiring the red gloves
It's a good thing you're here
and that you're listening to me

We are a conspiracy
stretching her arms out as far as possible
Tell the librarian
that I don't want any more atlases
tell him I want to read again
Now I'm interested in the novels of the twentieth century
remember that tell the librarian
that now I'm interested in twentieth-century novels
Those atlases threw my whole night
out of kilter
There I was arriving in Portugal
with a pile of luggage
and no one to help me
without you to help me Johanna
or in Switzerland or Turkey
it doesn't matter where
or else I see myself walking
pounding the pavement all the time
And giving the mailman a run for his money

CURTAIN

Second Prologue

After the ball. **The Good Woman** *in the costume of a queen.* **Johanna** *is wheeling her round the room ever faster, ever faster and faster, ecstatic.*
The Good Woman
Stop stop
Stand still
Johanna *stops the wheelchair*
The Good Woman
Wheel me back
Wheel me back to my place
Johanna *wheels her diagonally across the whole stage*
The Good Woman
I'm tired now
I am tired
now
What's the time

don't tell me what time it is
I can't stand so many people
I can't stand so many people any more
How many were there
These balls are always the same
Always the same people
always the same bad air
more and more people
How many were there actually
No other queen
I was the only queen
Most of them are ridiculous
no imagination
I was afraid that it would hurt me
when you took my costume off for me
it did hurt me
When you put it on for me
I was afraid of taking it off
I am afraid of taking it off
A dreadful costume
The band played off-key
nobody knows how to dance
The whole thing is
People think it's enough
to be stuck there in a costume
oh how these costume balls have changed
My costume caused me dreadful pain
the whole time
But today I don't want to go to bed any more
Tuesday is the party for Boris
Tuesday
Did you recognize the Chief Justice of the Constitutional Court
the Chief Justice of the Administrative Court
the wife of the Chief Justice of the Constitutional Court
the wife of the Chief Justice of the Administrative Court
The politicians
The doctors
Lawyers
The clerics
The Secretary of the Interior
The man who fell down
was the Foreign Minister

Johanna
The Foreign Minister

The Good Woman

    The Herr Prime Minister
    and the Frau Prime Minister
    the Frau Doctor
    the Frau Foreign Minister
    the Frau Secretary of the Interior
    How they came crowding in
    for the food
    The way people gorge themselves
    Now you know how
    people gorge themselves
    what they're like
    Don't ever leave me on my own again
    Suddenly you were gone
    You were dancing
    admit that you were dancing
    You must never again leave me on my own
    You must not be bamboozled
    You have to stay with me
    at my side
    stay
    But what's the time
    Who was I they asked
    and I said The Queen
setting her crown straight
    The whole time I demonstrated painlessness
    the whole time painlessness
    under this crown
    under this heavy crown
    throughout the whole ball
    I didn't once take it off

Johanna

    No one recognized you

The Good Woman

    No one not a soul
    they didn't recognize me
    me
    the Queen
setting her crown straight
    I'll keep it on
    This head Johanna
    One representation
    among nothing but representations
    This costume is much too heavy for me

You talked me into wearing this costume
You put the idea into my head
I did not want to go to the costume party
You forced me to
Wheel me a little way
wheel me quickly

Johanna *wheels her a little way*

The Good Woman
Quick
quick
Stop
Stand still
Open the curtains
Open them open them

Johanna *opens the curtains,* **The Good Woman** *notices that Johanna is*
no longer wearing a mask on her face

The Good Woman
Wheel me back
to my place

Johanna *wheels her back*

The Good Woman
But what have you done with your mask
Why pray do you not have your mask on your face any longer
Put it back on again at once
That's an order
put your mask on at once
I hadn't even noticed that you had taken off
your mask
And when did you take it off
How long is it since you stopped wearing it
You chose the lightest one for yourself
And I have this heavy crown on
this heavy crown
I have this costume on
I still have it on
You took your mask off

exit **Johanna**

The Good Woman *shouting after her*
You put on the lightest one
the lightest of all

Johanna *returns, now wearing a pig's head*

The Good Woman
You took it off behind my back
Didn't I tell you

that you had to ask my permission
if you wanted to take it off
You'll wear your mask as long as I wear my costume
Wheel me a little way
wheel me just a little way
Johanna *wheels her a little way*
The Good Woman
You picked out your mask yourself
The truth is that you picked out your mask
yourself
while I was forced by you into
this costume
this crown
forced to put this heavy chain
round my neck
Weeping with pain Johanna weeping
laughing
weeping with pain
this crown
this chain
this pain
But that was the way I wanted everything to be
so tight
so heavy
setting her crown straight
It's ridiculous
I wept
Suddenly having to play
the Weeping Woman
The Weeping Woman weeping under her crown
The whole time I was thinking
shall I take this costume off
or not
and I was thinking
shall I take this crown off
or not
This weakness
I'm incapable of action
incapable of action
while I am tortured by these thoughts
you behind my back
secretly take off your mask
But didn't you swear to me
that you would keep your mask on until

I gave you permission
to take it off
You took advantage of me
I let you out of my sight
and you took advantage of me
Out of my sight
out of my sight for a whole hour
took advantage
so adroitly that I didn't notice it
Took your mask off
Why didn't I notice it
This state of exhaustion
What
taking your mask out
didn't you just bring it in

Johanna *wheels her a little way*
The Good Woman
People keep trying again and again
Costume balls
Parties balls
are the saddest affairs
I did go
these balls
allow me to see those people
all together at the same time
A queen without legs
feigning a special privilege
Do you think that anyone recognized me
The Herr Secretary of the Interior
The Foreign Minister
The Chaplain did recognize me
The Chief of Police
But I did laugh out loud a few times
you have to admit that
that I laughed out loud
playing a queen who has no legs
a pathetic person
hits upon a pathetic idea
and enables other pathetic people
No
But if I had played myself
in that state of sudden ruthlessness
if I had played myself exactly
the way I play myself at home every day

and if you had had to play along with me
I would have forced you to play along with me
If the two of us our limbs
with all the malice of our heads
and our bodies
had had the courage to play me
and I had forced you to play along with me
I was unnoticed the whole time
observing the two of us
unnoticed Johanna
You always wanted to go off
to the men
But I didn't allow you into the ballroom
My torture is a far greater torture
My crown
Your pig's head
You heard that the ball
served a good cause
like all balls
Do you remember the ape
the ape
that I spoke to
that sudden conversation with the ape
The ape recognized me
the only one to recognize me at once the ape
the Chaplain
the ape is our Chaplain
I promised him a lot of money
for a good cause Johanna
Sacrifice
sacrifice
I said
and he
Sacrifice
and I
This great need and
Why is it that the need is so great
And he this need
all in whispers Johanna
for a good cause
in whispers
The ape and I
Chaplain I whispered This need
and he This need

The Queen was whispering with an ape about need
whispering about the good cause
When a queen whispers with an ape
then it costs a lot of money
Wheel me a little way

Johanna *wheels her a little way*

The Good Woman
We have gone among the apes
The Queen went about among the apes
accompanied by a pig
I am tired
Wheel me back to where I was

Johanna *wheels her back to the window*

The Good Woman
Open the curtains

Johanna *pretends to draw the curtains which have long been open*

The Good Woman
is my husband asleep
I asked whether my husband is asleep
is Boris asleep

Johanna
Yes

The Good Woman
We were at the ball
he was asleep
On Tuesday he shall have his party
Wake him up

exit **Johanna**

The Good Woman
He's asleep
he sleeps incessantly
I can't sleep

shouting through the open door
He must not come in
Not yet
Wash him
Comb his hair

to herself, exhausted
I won't
no
won't
This incessant
eating and sleeping

out loud
>Johanna
>wash his neck
>face and neck
>Put on his robe
>I don't want you to wash him from top to bottom
>it'll do if you just wipe him with a wet cloth
>No fuss
>Come
>Have you wiped his face
>Come here

to herself
>I cannot be alone
>I can't bear being alone any longer
>These tortures
>these frightful tortures

shouting
>Johanna Johanna

softly again
>Because for years I haven't been able to bear being alone

Johanna *enters*

The Good Woman
>You're taking advantage of this situation
>You take advantage of it
>when you wash him
>Wheel me a little way

Johanna *wheels her a little way*

The Good Woman
>What's the point of talking to him
>apart from the fact
>that he has no mind
>he has that foul smell
>But didn't I
>Didn't I select him for myself after all

to Johanna
>We went to the home and selected him for ourselves
>And I married him
>him
>him
>Say that we selected him for ourselves
>You forced me
>He feels nothing
>he is nothing and he feels nothing

He knows nothing
My creature
Why do I put up with these creatures
You were the one who put that idea into my head
I can still hear the Chaplain
Take he said
the most wretched one
the ugliest
My husband Johanna is our creature
You carried him out of the home for me
carried him down the steps
through the park into the car
The way you carried him
wrapped him up in sheets
combed his hair and put him in the car
All those creatures
As if he were your creature
But that creature it's mine alone
Boris belongs to me alone

exit **Johanna**

The Good Woman *shouting after her*
Did he resist when you washed him
I can't hear anything
usually he wants out
when you've washed him
Johanna

to herself
why can't I hear anything

out loud
You haven't given him an apple I hope
this early in the day
that's outrageous
You're not to give him apples
no apples during the reading
it's distracting
Give him something soundless to eat
something completely soundless
Wheel me
wheel me a little way

Johanna *enters and wheels her a little way*

The Good Woman
If you undress me now
everything will be still worse
if I give in now

sinking for a moment under the weight of the crown
    If I can just overcome this moment
suddenly sitting up very straight
    Was he startled
laughing repeatedly
    He was not startled
    He saw your pig's head
    and wasn't startled
    I'm cold
Boris *offstage whimpering*
    Johanna Johanna
The Good Woman *softly to Johanna*
    You mustn't bring him out
    until I give you permission
    Wait
    Listen
Boris
    Johanna
    Johannaaaaaaa
The Good Woman
    Did you tell him that we were at the ball
    He didn't ask you
    He didn't say anything
    He wasn't startled
    This pig's head
    If you take it off
Boris
    Johannaaaaaaa
Johanna *turns to bring him in*
The Good Woman
    Don't you dare
    Stay
    quiet
    He's getting scared
Boris
    Johannaaaaaaaaaaaaaaaa
The Good Woman
    He wants you
    to bring him out
    He wants to sit by the window
    and look out
    over to the home
    He wants to see the home
    He wants to go to his place by the window

Listen
is it still dark in his room
Johanna
Didn't you tell me
not to raise the blinds
He is afraid
The Good Woman
He is afraid
he is afraid
Boris *as though weeping*
Johannaaaaaaaaaaaaaaaa
The Good Woman
He's calling for *you*
not for *me*
for *you*
It's *you* he's calling
He's never called for *me*
Not one single time
not once
Boris
Johannaaaaaaaaaaaaaaaa
The Good Woman
Go on fetch him out
Bring him here
wheel him to the window
Johanna *exits*
The Good Woman *laughing*
I've had all the trees in the park cut down
so that he can see the home
from which I rescued him
Johanna *wheels* **Boris** *in, to the window, out of which he looks until
the curtain has fallen*
The Good Woman *to Boris*
Can you see the home
Boris *nods*
The Good Woman
You were afraid
Admit that you were afraid
You were afraid
Johanna tell him that last night
while he was fast asleep
we were at the charity ball
tell him that I was at the ball

in the mask of a queen
You were a pig
Tell him that
Johanna
But he just heard what you said
didn't he
The Good Woman
I said
that you were to tell it to him
I order you to tell it to him
Johanna *to Boris*
Madame says
that last night
The Good Woman
while he was fast asleep
Johanna
while you were fast asleep
we were at the costume ball
and that madame
The Good Woman
was in the costume of a queen
Johanna
was in the costume of a queen
The Good Woman
And that you
Johanna
and that I
The Good Woman
went as a pig
Johanna
and that I went as a pig
The Good Woman
as is proved by your mask
Johanna
as is proved by my mask
The Good Woman
that you were at the ball
Johanna
that I was at the ball
The Good Woman
as a pig
Johanna
as a pig

The Good Woman
   at the charity ball
Johanna
   at the charity ball
The Good Woman
   For charitable purposes tell him
   and that during the ball
   I thought of him
   Go on tell him
Johanna
   Madame thought of you
   during the ball
The Good Woman
   One single time
   and that one single time with horror
Johanna
   One single time
   and she thought of you with horror that one single time
The Good Woman *to Boris*
   Can you see the home
   Do you want to go back to the home
Boris *shakes his head*
The Good Woman *to Johanna*
   Leave us alone
   Make his bed
   Wash his caps
exit **Johanna**
The Good Woman
   These costume balls serve a purpose
   This crown I'm wearing is heavy
   On Tuesday your friends from the home are coming over
   Can you see the home
Boris *nods*
The Good Woman
   Your birthday
   the party for you
   How do you like my costume
   this crown
   How much this crown has cost me
   This crown
   don't you like this crown
   it's the most expensive costume that I have ever worn
   to the charity ball
   Can you see the home

Boris *nods*
Johanna *enters with a tray full of food and places it on* **Boris's** *lap: he starts eating at once and does not stop*
The Good Woman
Food
to Boris
Now you're to tell me
what you have read
didn't I order you to read the seventh chapter
What's in the seventh chapter
wheel me over to him Johanna
Johanna *wheels her to him*
The Good Woman *holding her crown*
What's in the seventh chapter
Johanna open the curtains
open them
open them all the way
Johanna *pulls at the open curtains*
The Good Woman *to Boris*
I don't want to torment you
I see that I am tormenting you
but I also see that you haven't read
the seventh chapter
I'm sure you haven't read it
But can't you see the home
to Johanna
You ought to part his hair
Wheel me back to where I was
Johanna *wheels her away from the window*
The Good Woman
Why isn't his hair parted
I thought I ordered you to part his hair
Why isn't his hair parted
Boris
I don't want my hair parted
The Good Woman *to Boris*
I want you to have your hair parted
to Johanna
Part his hair in the middle
Boris
I don't want my hair parted
The Good Woman
Part it in the middle
Boris *defiantly takes an apple out of his pocket and takes a bite*

The Good Woman *horrified*
   He has an apple an *apple*
Johanna *takes the apple away from him and puts it in her pocket*
The Good Woman
   Make sure that he never gets hold
   of an apple
   I can't stand the sound of him biting into an apple
to Boris
   Are you enjoying your food Boris
Boris *nods*
The Good Woman
   Open the windows Johanna
   I'm suffocating
Johanna *opens all the windows, then exits*
The Good Woman *to Boris*
   How old were you when you stole something for the first time
   three or four
Boris
   Three
The Good Woman
   There's a great difference
   stealing for the first time at age three and doing it at age four
   stealing
   repeat after me
   You must repeat after me
   There is a great difference
Boris
   There is a great difference
The Good Woman
   Who else in your family stole
   Oh well
   The ball has completely exhausted me
   This heavy crown
   Fancy my rescuing you from the home
laughing
   Boris
   were you the only one in your family who stole
   you must try to remember
   even if it's hard for you
   I have to know
   so you were the only one
   Were you the only one
Boris *shakes his head*

The Good Woman
> They all stole
> They all steal
> They didn't tell you
> Is it true that in the home
> they call me The Good Woman
> Is that the truth
> am I right that that is the truth

Boris *nods*

The Good Woman
> All of them

Boris *nods*

The Good Woman
> Not only you stole
> all of them all of them steal

Johanna *enters with a book, gives it to* **The Good Woman**

The Good Woman *leafing through the book*
to Boris
> Today's first test
> I know how far you read yesterday
> I can smell it Boris
> Here it is
> this is the place you read to
> You claim that you've read the seventh chapter as well
> You didn't even get as far as the sixth
> tell me what's on the last page of the sixth chapter
> You don't know
> How dare you
> Boris
> This meaningful ending
> I'll tell you what's at the end of the seventh chapter
> He did away with himself
> First he did away with her
> then he did away with himself
> When you lie you disgust me
> I know why I always make you give me a summary of the plot

giving the book to **Johanna**
> The tailor is coming at nine in the morning
> he'll measure you for a new pair of trousers
> and a new jacket
> You must have a white jacket
> to match my white gloves on Tuesday
> white trousers to match my white hat

So that we both match your friends from the home
looking into Johanna's face
    She likes you
    You like only her
    The tailor will measure you for a pair of white trousers
    a white jacket with pointed buttons
    the buttons are black and pointed
to Boris
    Can you see the home
    Would you like to go back to the home
Boris *shakes his head*
The Good Woman *to Johanna*
screaming
    Take off your mask
    Take off your mask
Johanna *takes off her mask*

CURTAIN

The Party

To the left a table, on it presents which can be clearly distinguished: a
    drum with a drumstick, a streamer, a clarinet, a rattle, a bottle of
    mead, a hat, a book, a stuffed raven, a jump rope, a telescope, a
    large dish of apples, a pair of officer's black boots, two pairs of
    long underpants, a red necktie. In the middle a long table, at
    which the Good Woman, Johanna—now also legless—and
    thirteen legless cripples are seated in wheelchairs; as the curtain
    rises they are celebrating Boris's birthday, eating, drinking,
    smoking, laughing. A fat waiter and a thin waiter serving them
    in silence, a fat attendant and a thin attendant watching over
    them in silence.
Young Cripple
    Go on go on
Old Cripple
    Swine

Two Cripples
    Go on go on
The Oldest Cripple *narrating*
    Now comes the gloom
almost singing
    Now comes the darkness
    the darkness
Three Cripples
    The gloom
    The darkness
Young Cripple
    Don't interrupt don't interrupt
Old Cripple
    The darkness
Four Cripples
    The darkness
The Oldest Cripple
    Big very big heads
    in the darkness
    You must picture it for yourselves
    very big heads
    in the darkness
    suddenly the biggest heads were there
Six Cripples *laugh*
The Oldest Cripple
    Why are you laughing
    It's not laughable
    there's nothing to laugh about
Six Cripples *laugh*
The Oldest Cripple
    Nothing
    Laugh
    There's nothing to laugh about
out loud
    It's not a comedy
Boris *laughs*
The Oldest Cripple
    Who's that laughing
    Who laughed just now
Three Cripples
    Boris laughed
    Boris
The Good Woman *to Boris*
    Why did you laugh

There's nothing to laugh about
did you hear
there's nothing to laugh about
did you hear
nothing
The Oldest Cripple
Nothing Nothing
The Good Woman
It's not laughable
Young Cripple
Go on go on
All *in a confusion of voices*
Go on
The Oldest Cripple
Something gloomy
it is gloomy
it is dark
The big heads had no ears
the big heads had no eyes
the big heads had no noses
the big heads had no feet
All *laugh*
All *in a confusion of voices*
No eyes
no ears
no noses
no feet
The Oldest Cripple
No eyes
they saw nothing
no ears
they heard nothing
no noses nothing
no sense
nothing
And no hair
All *laugh*
Two Cripples
No hair
Two Other Cripples
So they were bald
Old Cripple
Bald
Young Cripple *laughs*

All *laugh*
The Oldest Cripple
    But they had big mouths
    the biggest heads had the biggest mouths
Two Cripples *laugh*
All *laugh*
The Youngest Cripple
    Where was it
The Oldest Cripple
    In the gloom
    In the darkness
The Good Woman
    Eat eat come on eat
    eat
    you must eat everything up
    eat it up eat everything up drink everything up
    eat eat up eat
Cripple
    In the darkness
Cripple *to him*
    Shut your trap
Cripple
    I dreamed
Cripple *to him*
    Shut your trap
Cripple
    I had to eat everything up
    that's what I dreamed
Cripple *to him*
    Shut your trap
Cripple
    I had a dream too
Old Cripple
    Swine
All *laugh*
The Oldest Cripple
    Filthy pig
The Good Woman *to Johanna*
    It's painful
    everything is painful and everything hurts
    But for you the whole thing is just a pretense
    you know that just for today you're pretending
    that you have no legs any longer
    while I have no legs

you are just pretending
that you have no legs
if you really didn't have legs any longer
I had you strapped in
tied up
strapped in and tied up
so that you will fit the occasion
so that you will fit in with all the rest of us
now none of us has any legs
none of us
do you understand
you too don't have legs any longer
do you understand
no
you don't understand
you understand nothing
you understand everything
and understand nothing
today you have to be suited to the occasion
pretend
that you don't have legs
no one must stand out
everyone must be the same
everyone the same
everything the same
Now you have legs
and yet don't have legs
don't have legs
and yet you do have legs
and understand nothing
and it hurts you
not to have legs and yet to have legs
it pains you more than it pains me
more
you feel more pain
the greatest pain
the cruel pain
cruel
I forced you
to hide your legs
Don't forget our agreement
as long as the party goes on
you have to hide your legs
be without legs

do you understand
you have hidden your legs
you are strapped in
exhausted
everything is cruel
you are strapped in
you can't run away
you can't
Hey waiter waiter
eat eat drink drink
everybody drink everybody eat
do eat Johanna eat
drink

Cripple
Good
Cripple
Good
The Good Woman
It's good to eat
it's good to drink
everything's good
All *in a confusion of voices*
Good
everything is good
good good good
The Good Woman
Eat drink
drink eat
Old Cripple
The Good Woman is a lady
Young Cripple
The lady is good
The Oldest Cripple
But I didn't only dream about the big heads
about the biggest heads
I was walking
and next to me someone else was walking next to me
and was telling me over and over he was telling me
that I had to read something by him
an author
read something
over and over he said I should read something
by him read something read something by him
mercilessly

read he said
read he kept saying
read read
the whole time read read
Pause
Then I did away with him
Cripple
And how did you do that
The Oldest Cripple
Beat him to death
Old Cripple
Beat him to death
he beat him to death beat him
Young Cripple
Where was that
The Oldest Cripple
In the darkness
The Good Woman
Eat eat
Waiter waiter
Johanna cut up the cakes
cut
Waiter waiter
fill the glasses eat
Young Cripple
I dreamed about a bunny
Old Cripple
Shut your trap
Young Cripple *to him*
Leave him alone
Old Cripple *to him*
Shut your trap
Young Cripple
About his bunnies
Young Cripple
My bunnies
Old Cripple
Shut your trap
pointing at The Oldest Cripple
The Oldest Cripple
And in my dream
mind you my legs
were so long
that I could look into the fourth floor

the fourth floor is the most interesting
there are some who think
the third
and there are some who think
the ground floor is the most interesting
the fourth floor is the most interesting
not the fifth either
and not the sixth
the fourth
the floor where the intelligentsia live
the most interesting people live on the fourth floor
dwell
those who have brains
those who have imagination
my legs were so long that I could look into the fourth floor
legs so long that there wouldn't have been room for them
in this salon
even in this large splendid salon
Unless I had let the lot of you
break them to bits for me

Young Cripple

I had a dream that I saw someone digging
and I says what are you doing
and he says: digging
and I says how long have you been at it
and he says: I'm digging
and I says what's the point
and he says: I'm digging
and how deep are you digging
and he says: until I get through

All *laugh*

The Good Woman

Eat eat
These giant cakes

All *in a confusion of voices*

The best pieces of cake
the best

The Good Woman *moving a large piece toward herself*

That's a piece
an especially large piece
What a piece
Johanna what a piece of cake
Stop
Who's to have this big piece

who
I've never in my life seen such a big piece
who of you has ever seen such a big piece of cake
All *in a confusion of voices*
A large piece
The Good Woman
Let's give it to the hungriest
Who is the hungriest
Whose hunger is the greatest
Which of you is the hungriest
It's true you've been eating for two hours already
but one of you is still the hungriest
very hungry big piece of cake
laughs
No
not the one whose hunger is the greatest
shall have it
but he who deserves it
only he who deserves it
looking at them one after the other, then
No one
not one of us
not a single one deserves this piece
I shall cut it up and distribute it
I shall cut it into as many pieces as there are people here
But how many of us are there actually
All *counting out loud in a confusion of voices*
The Good Woman
Stop
I'll count
counting
One two three four five six seven eight nine
ten eleven twelve thirteen fourteen fifteen sixteen
With Johanna and Boris we are sixteen
to Boris
with you Boris we are sixteen
If the Chaplain were here we'd be seventeen
but the Chaplain has broken his foot
All *in a confusion of voices*
Broke his foot
the Chaplain
broke his foot
broke

The Good Woman
> The Chaplain broke his foot
> while he was talking to me on the telephone
> If you have a foot
> you can break it
> If you've got one
> If you haven't got a foot
> If you don't have one
> you can't break it

Three Cripples *laugh*
Old Cripple
> This is good food

The Good Woman
> Broke his foot

Old Cripple
> Wouldn't you say Ludwig Viktor
> that this is good food

Young Cripple *to his neighbor*
> Eat eat

Two Cripples
> Isn't there fennel in this

All *in a confusion of voices*
> Anise and fennel

Oldest Cripple *pointing to the youngest*
> He had a dream last night
> that he had stuffed his head
> with straw

Old Cripple
> Dreams are important

All *laugh*
Old Cripple
> Tedious isn't it
> Karl Ludwig
> tedious

The Good Woman
> Eat eat

Young Cripple
> I once ate my soup
> with my feet
> in a dream

The Youngest Cripple
> And I wrote a long letter
> with my legs

which I don't have
Old Cripple
  With his own feet
to the Youngest Cripple
  Or is it not true
  that last night with your own feet
  you wrote a long letter
  to the director of the home
to The Good Woman
  A letter of complaint
to the Youngest Cripple
  And what was in the letter
to The Good Woman
  He's embarrassed
to the Youngest Cripple
  You're embarrassed
  to say here and now
  what you wrote in the letter to the director of the home
to The Good Woman
  A letter of complaint dear lady
  Good woman
  he wrote
  that the bed he sleeps in is too short for him
  he wants a longer bed
All *in a confusion of voices*
  Yes yes
  we all want longer beds
  have a longer bed
Old Cripple *to The Good Woman*
  He wants a longer bed
to the Youngest Cripple
  How long are you Ernst August
  Tell us how long you are
The Youngest Cripple
  One eighty
Old Cripple
  One eighty *with* legs
  How long are you *without* legs
The Youngest Cripple
  Eighty one
Older Cripple
  He's eighty one *without* legs
  He was one eighty *with* legs
  One eighty minus ninety nine

is eighty one
And how long is your bed
The Youngest Cripple
Seventy one
Old Cripple *to The Good Woman*
It's a tragedy madame
Cripple
My bed is too short too
Cripple
Mine too
Cripple
I can't stretch out either
Cripple
I sleep in a bed
which is one—o—four long
but I am one—o—eight long
Cripple
I am sixty long
and my bed is fifty eight long
All *in a confusion of voices*
We all have beds which are too short
Bodies too long
for those short beds
Cripple
I've never been able to stretch
my torso out in my bed
The Good Woman
I shall see to it
that you get longer beds
everyone must have a bed in which he can stretch out
I should think that's the very least you can ask for
to be able to stretch out in your own bed
it's ridiculous that you can't stretch out
in your beds
A disgrace
A disgrace to the institution
a disgrace to the home
a disgrace to the director of the institution
a disgrace to this country
It really is absurd
All *look reproachfully at one another*
The Good Woman
Complain
You must complain

resist
rebel
protest
Boris has
looking at Boris
    Boris has a long bed
    in which he can stretch himself out
    I should think that's the very least he can ask of me
    to give him a bed in which he can stretch himself out
to Boris
    Isn't that right
    you can stretch yourself out in your bed
Boris *nods*
The Good Woman
    Tell your friends
    that you can stretch yourself out
    whenever you like
    Except that he never stretches himself out
    Never
    I know that he never stretches himself out
    but if he wants to stretch himself out
    he can stretch himself out
    He has my first husband's bed
    He was one ninety
to Boris
    Tell them that you can stretch yourself out in your bed
    if you want to
Boris *nods*
The Good Woman
    He eats and sleeps
    that's it
    I don't know anybody
    who sleeps as well
    and eats as much
Cripple
    My lady you must admit that it's sad
    not to be able to stretch yourself out in your own bed
Cripple
    It's scandalous
Cripples
    Scandalous
All *in a confusion of voices*
    Scandalous

Cripple
   To have to sleep in beds that are much too short
The Oldest Cripple
   To have to sleep
to The Good Woman
   and not be able to stretch yourself out
   You know yourself what it's like
   when you don't have legs any longer
   And when you don't have legs any longer
   and cannot stretch yourself out at night
Cripple
   The director of the home saves wood at our expense
Cripple
   And nails
Cripple
   And glue
Cripple
   Money
Two Cripples
   Bed linen and mattresses
Cripple
   We sleep in beds
   which are on an average ten to twenty centimeters too short for us
Cripple
   Which are ten to forty centimeters shorter
   than our bodies
Cripple
   Torsos
Four Cripples
   Torsos torsos torsos
All *in a confusion of voices*
   Scandalous
Cripple
   I constantly feel the need
   to stretch myself out
   and cannot stretch myself out
Cripple
   We do not lie in beds
   we lie in boxes
The Oldest Cripple *laughing*
   That's a good one: in boxes
Cripple
   It's true

Cripple
Dear lady it's true
All
In boxes in boxes
Cripple
Whoever's unlucky enough
to have a body which is too large
and most of us have bodies which are too large
My friend Ernst August has an especially large body
he had short unsightly legs
between you and me my dear lady he was bandy-legged
but as you can see for yourself a body which is too large much too larg
it's exactly the same in Karl Ludwig's case
and Ludwig Viktor
and Hans Ernst
and Ernst Ludwig
and Hans Viktor
and Karl Ludwig Viktor
The Oldest Cripple
All the beds are the same size
Cripple *correcting him*
Boxes boxes
The Oldest Cripple
All the boxes are the same size
Cripple *out loud*
Standard issue box
Two Cripples
Standard issue box
All
We sleep in standard issue boxes
The Oldest Cripple
The fact that I have less pain than anybody else is the result
of my having a small body myself
to The Good Woman
as you can see
from birth
All *laugh*
The Oldest Cripple *to The Good Woman*
As you can see madam
but I had very long legs
the longest legs in the family
My body is shockingly short
That was something which always caused me great suffering

as a child
until suddenly I didn't have legs any longer
until I went into the home
my family caused me great suffering
my parents and my siblings
they all kept saying if only he didn't have such long legs
if only he didn't have such a shockingly short body
that's what they said madam
now my shockingly short torso
makes life easier for me
everything
Those short beds
Cripple *correcting him*
Boxes
The Oldest Cripple
Those short boxes are scandalous
All *in a confusion of voices*
Scandalous
The Oldest Cripple
Now I'm in a much better position
I can stretch myself out
for me my bed
Cripple *correcting him*
Your box
The Oldest Cripple
My box is not too short for me
I have the advantage of having a shockingly short body
Before the accident
Cripple
Tell us how it happened
He tells it so well
Cripple
Tell us
The Oldest Cripple
I don't want to
Cripple
The lady wants to hear it
The Oldest Cripple
No
Cripple
He only tells the story on Friday
Today is Tuesday
It was in the war

The Good Woman
    In the war in the war
    But the others lost their legs
    after the war like me
    after the war
    Isn't that true
    all of you after the war
    Waiter waiter
    Who needs more coffee
Cripple
    I need more coffee
The Good Woman
    Johanna
    Ludwig August needs more coffee
Cripple
    I simply adopt this diagonal position
showing his diagonal position
    so that my bed
Cripple *correcting him*
    Your box
Cripple
    so that I fit into my box
    I have no pain at all in this diagonal position
showing his diagonal position once again
    Look here this is what it's like
    my diagonal position
Johanna *laughs*
The Good Woman
    Why are you laughing
    Why on earth are you laughing
Pause
Cripple
spitting out hot coffee on to the tablecloth
    Ouch that's hot
Old Cripple
    There are many methods
    of making life in the box
    more bearable
    Karl Ernst often sleeps standing up
    What a sight that is
Cripple
    Standing up
Old Cripple
    He has the best method

But of course there is no Best Method
You can't shorten your bodies any further
We can't commit suicide either
we often discuss it
the how and the when
when and how
The Oldest Cripple
We are always entertaining the thought of doing away with ourselves
Cripple
I am always thinking about it
Cripple
Always
Cripple
Indeed
Old Cripple
But we don't do it
If we did we'd have to do it en masse
all together
in a single moment
Cripple
At the same moment
mimes cutting his throat and hanging himself
The Oldest Cripple
But we don't do it
We think about it
we discuss it
but we don't do it
The Good Woman
I shall talk to the director of the home
so that you'll get longer beds
For my husband's birthday
I'm going to treat you to
longer beds
Two Cripples
Boxes, boxes
The Good Woman
My annual donation must be used for longer beds
that's the first priority
Agreed Johanna
they are all to get longer beds
beds they can stretch themselves out in
to Boris
do you hear
they are going to get longer beds from me

in which they can stretch themselves out
for your birthday
do you hear
Boris *nods*
The Good Woman
All right then longer beds
Waiter waiter
Two Cripples
Boxes
The Good Woman
Beds are always boxes
Waiter waiter The presents
After all the director of the home will listen to reason
The Waiters *fetch the presents from the table and pile them up in front
of Boris, the cripples murmur in astonishment. When all the
presents are piled up in front of* **Boris,** *the drum is nearest him
and he picks up the drumstick and beats on the drum three
times.*
The Good Woman
The drum is from Ernstludwig
Cripple *nods*
The Good Woman
The clarinet is from Ernstaugust
Cripple *nods*
The Good Woman
The streamer is from Karlernst
Cripple *nods*
The Good Woman
The rattle is from Ernstludwigaugust
The Good Woman
The bottle of mead is from Karlludwigviktor
Cripple *nods*
The Good Woman
The hat is from Karlviktor
Cripple *nods*
The Good Woman
The book is from Karlaugusternst
Cripple *nods*
The Good Woman
The stuffed raven is from Karlviktorernst
Cripple *nods*
The Good Woman
The jump rope is from Ernstaugustkarl
Cripple *nods*

The Good Woman
   The telescope is from Augustkarlviktor
Cripple *nods*
The Good Woman
   The apples are from Johanna
to Johanna
   Sadist
to Boris
   The officer's boots which you've always wanted
   are from me
   The long underpants are from me
   The red necktie is from the Chaplain
Boris *beats the drum three times*
The Good Woman
   Of course the drum
Boris *beats the drum three times*
The Good Woman
   The drum of course
Boris *beats the drum three times*
The Good Woman *to Boris*
   Go on beat the drum
Boris *beats the drum sixteen times, meanwhile*
The Oldest Cripple *to The Good Woman*
   We keep asking ourselves
   what form of suicide
   would be most bearable for us
Cripple
   Always with what
   and how to do it
Cripple
   with our bed sheets
   with our pocket knives
Cripple
   with the kitchen knives
Cripple
   or jump out of the window
Cripple
   We are constantly occupied with this thought
   There's no other thought in our minds
Cripple
   It's our one diversion
Cripple
   We don't do it
   but we discuss it

The Youngest Cripple
    I dreamed that I did it
    with my necktie
during this speech **Boris** *drinks from the bottle of mead*
    with a red tie
    and none of you noticed
The Oldest Cripple
    He dreams of nothing else
Cripple
    I'm always dreaming that
    I'm doing away with you all
Boris *plays with the rattle*
Cripple *to his neighbor*
    You're eating too much
The Good Woman
    Help yourselves help yourselves
    eat eat
    You must eat everything up
Boris *beats the drum six times*
The Good Woman *looking at him*
    The drum then
    Oh how I look forward to this party
    I look forward to this party all year
    to Boris's birthday
    and to you
    Waiter waiter
    My husband talks about you a lot
    even though he keeps most things secret from me
    he insists that all of you
    especially on Saturdays
    used to sing a song over and over again
    the song about the wagtail
Boris *takes the stuffed raven and lifts it up,* **The Good Woman** *recalls*
    the words of the song, she tries to sing it.
    In the dark in the dark
    it's not flown for many a day
    in the dark in the dark
    it's not flown for many a day
suddenly commanding
    sing it sing the song
    I want to hear the song
Cripples *all look at one another*
The Good Woman *sings the song*
Cripple *begins to sing*

Two Cripples *join in*
Six Cripples *join in*
All Cripples *sing softly, louder, then softly again*
    In the dark in the dark
    it's not flown for many a day
    in the dark in the dark
    it's not flown for many a day
Cripple
    Stop stop
    once again from the beginning
Boris *joins in and beats time almost inaudibly with the drumstick*
All
    In the dark in the dark
    it's not flown for many a day
    in the dark in the dark
    it's not flown for many a day
    it was perched on a little bough
    it was perched on a little bough
they break off the song
Cripple
    Can't do it on a full stomach
Boris *beats the drum four times as fast as possible*
The Oldest Cripple
    We're stuffed
    can't sing like that
Boris *beats the drum four times as fast as possible*
The Good Woman *humming*
    In the dark in the dark
Cripple *joins in*
The Oldest Cripple *to him*
    Shut your trap
to the Good Woman
    He can't sing
    he can't sing a note
    there are some among us
    who can't sing a note
    We sing my lady
    or we think about suicide
Boris *beats the drum four times as fast as possible*
The Good Woman
    Is it true that the beds at the home are bug-infested
The Oldest Cripple
    The truth dear lady
    it is true

there are bugs in the home
and the beds there are the most infested of all
it is the truth
The Good Woman
I didn't believe my husband
Boris *beats the drum four times as fast as possible*
Because the drum is all he has
to Boris
Isn't it true that I didn't
to the others
He eats every chance he gets
is it true that you are punished
if you complain
if you complain to the director of the home about the bugs
All *nod*
The Oldest Cripple
It's true my lady
We are allowed to complain
but it's no use
Cripple
No use
The Youngest Cripple
No use
The Good Woman
My husband never complained
isn't that true
my husband never complained
he would rather have been eaten alive
Boris *beats the drum four times as fast as possible*
The Good Woman *to Boris*
Isn't it true you'd rather have been eaten alive
Boris *beats the drum four times as fast as possible*
The Good Woman
Once he rebelled
against the barber
against the institution's barber
Cripple
The swine
All *in a confusion of voices*
The barber is a swine
Cripple
He hurts everyone
he cuts everybody in the face

in the ear
in the scalp
in the neck
in the chin
Cripple
Wherever he can
wherever he likes
The Good Woman
Barbers are all alike
Cripple
Like doctors
Cripple
Doctors are swine
All *in a confusion of voices*
Doctors are swine
The Attendants *take a pace forward*
All *in a confusion of voices*
Swine charlatans
charlatans charlatans
swine
doctors are swine and charlatans
The Youngest Cripple
Swine
The Good Woman
Remarkable
all that
is remarkable
All
Swine
charlatans
The Oldest Cripple
A new set of regulations for the home
is long overdue
All
A new set of regulations for the home
Boris *beats the drum sixteen times, four quick beats, two slow, and*
growing ever louder, meanwhile
Cripple
Thorough inspections every month
Cripple
Beginning at the top
Cripple
Thorough inspections

All *in a confusion of voices*
   Thorough inspections
   Inspections thorough ones
The Youngest Cripple
   Dismiss dismiss
All *in a confusion of voices and growing louder and louder*
   Dismiss dismiss
The Attendants *come closer*
All
   Dismiss dismiss
The Good Woman
   Quiet quiet
Boris *beats the drum sixteen times, four times fast, two slow, and*
      growing ever louder, meanwhile
The Good Woman
   Quiet quiet
All
   Dismiss dismiss
   better food
   clean bed linen
   new wheelchairs
   new wheelchairs
   new wheelchairs
Cripple
   More nurses
   fewer lazy doctors
Cripple
   Doctors are lazy
Cripple
   Swine
All *in a confusion of voices*
   New wheelchairs
   More opportunities for exercise
   better medication
   exercise
Cripple
   We must have a new barber
Boris *beats the drum louder and louder*
All *in a confusion of voices*
   A new surgeon
   a new surgeon
   dismiss
The Good Woman
   Quiet quiet

but isn't there any entertainment at all in the home
don't you have any people to give recitals
no dancers no writers
visiting lecturers
conjurors clairvoyants
doesn't the home engage any people to give recitals
It's often enough to have someone who reads aloud
or makes a pigeon disappear or a dog
for a depression
or dreadful depressions
Boris *beats the drum even more loudly*
The Good Woman *shouting*
    It helps me to get over the most difficult situations
    if I listen to the woman who reads aloud to me
looking at Johanna
    listen Johanna
    I can imagine that if now and again
    if now and again a comic
Boris *beats the drum still more loudly*
The Good Woman
    an especially comic or especially clever person
    were to come to the home
Cripple
    We don't need artists
    We don't need recitalists
The Good Woman
    Yes but
Boris *beats the drum even more loudly*
The Oldest Cripple
    We need better food
    longer beds
    improvements in our general condition
    no artists
    no clever people dear lady
    my dear lady
    we make our own fun for ourselves
    and we devise our own philosophical systems
All *nod*
Boris *beats the drum even more loudly twelve times very fast and*
    slumps forward, without anyone's noticing it, with his head on to
    the table like a corpse
The Oldest Cripple
    Ludwigviktor for example
    can make himself disappear

he simply vanishes
you can't see him any more nothing
he's simply disappeared
when he whistles his whistle
he calls it his disappearance whistle
or Ernstaugust
who simply doubles himself
or can even triple himself if he has too
You wouldn't believe your eyes my lady
to Ernstludwigviktor
Hey Ernstludwigviktor show the lady your trick
show her that you don't have just one head on your shoulders but
four
four identical ones or at least indistinguishable ones
come on show the lady your trick
Cripple *shakes his head*
The Oldest Cripple
He doesn't want to
it's no use if he doesn't want to
he says it's no use
whenever he has four heads he says that he feels
and of course that's understandable
four times the pain
four heads ache four times as much as one head
even a simple headache is enough to drive him to distraction
And now imagine that dear lady multiplied by four
never mind Ernstludwigviktor
it's a never-ending source of surprise to us all that there's room on
him for all four of his heads
when even one on its own is much too heavy for him
He's surprised himself
No madam we make our own fun for ourselves
But madam what Ludwigkarlernst does
well I'd rather not say
or Karlviktorernst
Without any pain at all he cuts his
No madam no
or Karlludwigernst
no madam no
Boris always gave us the feeling for a few moments
that we had legs
but he didn't always succeed
that feat demanded superhuman concentration on his part
Sometimes when we wanted it

we waited for this feeling
in vain
Karlaugust tricks us into thinking that he is our king
we can see a crown on his head
and we agree that his nose
suits his chubby royal cheeks very well
Ernstaugust often calls himself Duke
Karlviktor often says Schweinehund
who grunts and barks his life away
or we tell one another
when we don't have colic that is
or digestive troubles or other bodily malfunctions
about the mistakes we have made
the errors in judgment which led
to our not having any legs any longer dear lady
Karlludwig lost his in France
Karlaugust in England
Ernstludwig in Ireland
I lost mine on the main square in Paderborn
Ernstludwigaugust's were cut off by doctors
in an excruciating procedure
my case is a similar case
a dog a wolfhound
which belonged to the manager of a Nuremberg apartment building
bit me in both legs
the doctors had to take them off
within three days
and what's more it was during the Foehn[1]
I only noticed it three weeks later
when I came round
from the anesthetic

Cripple
From the anesthetic

The Oldest Cripple
A nice game is the game we play
called Gofaraway
if we're in England
we speak English
if we're in France

---

1. The Foehn is a wind which blows from the Alps and is frequently regarded as the cause
of a number of minor and unspecified bodily disorders. In Munich (they say) the doctors
don't like to operate when the Foehn is blowing.

French
what else
or we imitate dogs
and bark our time away
or cows
and allow ourselves to be milked
The most educated one among us after me is without doubt
Ernstludwigviktor
he quotes all the great literature to us
right up to the present day
until we tell him to shut his trap
But Karlernst madam always does the best trick
he cuts his head off in front of us
and boxes its ears in mid-air
until we can't stand watching him any longer
then he says when he puts it back on again
that he has a new head on once again
and understands life better
seeing that all are now tired
to The Good Woman
Madam everything
as you can see has been eaten up
besides which fatigue has seized every one of us
yawning
fatigue you see
I think it's time we were going
All *nudge one another*
Cripple
Good food
The Oldest Cripple *to The Good Woman*
Good food and drink madam
a lovely birthday
Whenever people talk about you
they always talk about the Good Woman
never anything but the Good Woman
to them all
Say thank you
say thank you to the lady
say to the lady thank you
All *in a confusion of voices*
Thank you thank you
thank you thank you
Cripple *shakes Boris*

The Oldest Cripple
    Boris
Cripple *shakes Boris several times*
All *look at Boris*
Johanna *suddenly*
    He's dead
screaming
    He's dead
to The Good Woman
    He's dead
    Boris is dead
exeunt **All** *with the exception of* **The Good Woman,** *either wheeling*
    themselves in their wheelchairs or being wheeled in silence by
    the attendants and waiters and backing out of the room. Hardly
    is The Good Woman alone with Boris's corpse when she bursts
    into horrible peals of laughter.

THE END

A WORD ABOUT *RITTER, DENE, VOSS*

The title of the play is actually the names of three famous German actors, Ilse Ritter, Kirsten Dene, and Gert Voss. As the reviewer in *Theater Heute* says, "This play is a continuation of Bernhard's Comédie Misanthropique." With reference to the note at the end of the play, it may be pointed out that genuinely biographical incidents in the lives of both Ludwig Wittgenstein and of his nephew Paul are conflated in the stage experiences of the character Voss.

As in all of Bernhard's plays, we are dealing with the thin line between sanity and insanity, between reality and fiction. The important thing about this play is that it should be played at a good pace and that the director and actors realize that the effects are gained from the verbal fireworks of the piece. This is not to say, of course, that several of Bernhard's favorite themes do not appear once again in this play. The corruptibility and the dictatorial ways of the medical profession—a central theme in *A Party for Boris*—is of course central here as well.

The social criticism here revolves around the parochialism and repetitiveness of Viennese upper-middle-class cultural life and the stultifying effect this has upon intellectual life. Yet we should not be led astray by the absurdities of the situations. Minetti, the actor whom Bernhard most admired on the German stage, says "I consider Bernhard to be a completely realistic and concrete writer." If we think of the works of Harold Pinter and the hyper-realism of a play like *The Caretaker* we may find some guidance in presenting the present play to an American audience.

RITTER, DENE, VOSS

They have always made us suffer
these hideous pictures

Mansion in Döbling

Dining Room

Dramatis Personae
Voss *is Ludwig*
Dene *his older sister*
Ritter *his younger sister*

Before Midday Dinner

View of a small kitchen (of a sort called a tea-kitchen in German, i.e.,
  a sort of butler's pantry with facilities for the brewing of tea etc.)
  with glass doors
A second door, a window
A sideboard, a large table and a small one
A number of armchairs
A tall lamp, an ornate grandfather's clock, a mirror, a record player
Large family portraits on the walls
Ritter *in an armchair at the window, smoking a cigarette*
Dene *comes out of the kitchen and begins to set the table*
  Bath too hot
  it's always the same with him
  difficulties of interpretation
  apathy
  catafalquism that's what he accuses us of
Ritter
  Did you tell him
  that Doctor Frege is the only possible one
Dene
  No I have to proceed carefully
  Proceed gently Fräulein Worringer
  the director said
Ritter
  The follow-up physician Doctor Frege

Dene
Between Steinhof and here
he hardly said a word hardly a word
Ritter
Not even about Schopenhauer
Dene
No
Ritter
And his Germanophobia
Dene
Not a word about the Germans
Ritter
And his sore throat
Dene
Better
he's not coughing any more
Not a word about Frege
I don't feel like kicking the bucket
to save my brother
that's what I told the director
looking under the table and continuing to set it
It's out of an instinct for self-preservation that I'm taking my brother
home
is what I said
I can't come to Steinhof every day
after all I'm not well myself
He looked at me uncomprehendingly
Do what you think is right he said
but don't forget that your brother
is extremely vulnerable
extremely vulnerable
Ritter
Pointless to think about the inadmissible
Dene
While you only visited him once a week
I went to Steinhof every day
Ritter
Day in day out
Dene
Destruction self-destruction philosophical
that's what he said
threw his salami sandwich into the toilet bowl
in front of my very eyes

Schopenhauer and washing his hands
Talked again about his log cabin in Sognefjord
going on about Norway in his room all the time
I didn't know how to get him off the subject
and only the day before the word *Germanophobia* all the time
Ritter
The Norwegian quirk
Dene *goes into the kitchen*
Ritter
Paid three million in two years
because we have no medical insurance
taking off her left shoe and tipping it out high above her head
Catafalquism
a stone falls out of her shoe
You ought to have left him in peace
have left him in Steinhof
Dene
But it's only a trial
Ritter
Which always ends in disaster
Dene
Tell me where are the sugar cubes?
Ritter *putting her shoe on again*
In the left-hand drawer
Dene
Got himself completely snowed in at Sils Maria
coming out of the kitchen and continuing to set the table
Burned all his Christmas presents
scornful laughter
shortage of breath afraid he was dying
Once again afraid of cancer of the tongue
Ritter
Cancer of the tongue is not hereditary
Dene
Yes it is
Ritter *who has picked up a newspaper and is reading*
How long has father been dead
Dene
Twenty years
Ritter
He had the most beautiful death
that I can imagine
without the slightest pain

he went to sleep like a child
Only two days before
we had been to the opera
Turandot

Dene

Henry James conceived us
not our parents
that's what he said
Smothered in luxury
always just *barely* got away

Ritter

You or I
to this very day
that will never change

Dene

I let him finish talking
Treatise on Logic Part One
Treatise on Logic Part Two
finally transcribed I said
all along the avenue
and back again
without contradicting
I said he should sit in the back seat
he didn't object at all
got in all by himself
the pills worked immediately
He wanted to go along Hill Road
we stopped at the Fischer House
he asked to get out
we got out
we took a short walk
he seemed quite calm
he looked down at the city
wanted to know where our house was
he couldn't find it at once
that annoyed him
There it is I said
that made him doubly annoyed
that *I* had found it before he had
I hadn't changed he said
And neither had you
sisters are the problem he said
then I saw

that he had no socks on
shoes on his bare feet
thanked me a second time for my typing
it was us father had loved he said
for him he only had hatred
suddenly he recited his favorite sentence
the Schopenhauer sentence
quite calmly without the least agitation
I'd arranged
I said
for us to be alone
when he got home
just us siblings
no servants
no maid
We really only need the small kitchen
nobody but ourselves
To take a bath by myself
he said
without being stared at
by a keeper
He wanted to go for a stroll
we walked a little way into the woods
I said I had been to the cemetery
the family grave was neglected
the birch tree had split the slab on the tomb
he was fascinated
that I should describe the grave to him
and how I did it
going into the kitchen
We simply have to take
our chances
One day you'll take a walk in the park with him
and I'll do it the next day
Ritter
I was against it
I'm still against it
I would never have taken him out
at least not at this moment
Dene
Now or never
I thought
Now he's agreed

Ritter
    You're totally absorbed in Ludwig
    you've organized your whole life around him
Dene
    With his consent
    do bear that in mind
coming out of the kitchen
    he wanted to come home now
Ritter
    I wouldn't have brought him home
    not now of all times
    Now that you're returning to the stage
    playing that blind woman
    it's ridiculous and you know it
Dene
    Precisely because I am returning to the stage
Ritter *reading*
    Self-realization
    what a disgusting word
    this odious word crops up everywhere
    self-realization
    there's nothing more repellent
    there's nothing more stupid
    it doesn't mean anything
    the word self-realization
    but they're all parroting it
    doesn't matter what or who you are
    you are after all realized
    and you are yourself
    there isn't a more absurd word
    there isn't a more repellent one
    than the word self-realization
    and everyone uses it continuously
    The phrase function of truth is another example
Dene
    I hate those words
    all those terms
    He said that we were intelligent siblings
looking at the clock
    Perhaps you'll go with him
    to Doctor Frege's
    tomorrow afternoon
Ritter
    He only says what he's thought *out*

Dene
  There always has to be fresh milk in the house
  that's important
  I'll go for a walk with him in the park
  every day
  I said to the director
  and I will be punctilious about his pills
  Be careful
  not to leave him on his own
  when he cuts his toenails
  the director said
  always hang his coats up
  so that the lining can't be seen
  You must take your time with him
  When he expounds his logic to you
  you must listen to him
  you must keep quiet
  no comments you understand
  no contradiction
  as if we didn't know him better than that
  and don't say
  that you haven't understood
  just as you mustn't say
  that you *have* understood
  What a repellent person that director is
  polish his glasses
  he said
  without his knowing
  and be sure to do it every day
  because he doesn't polish them and thinks
  he's bound to go blind
  he's afraid of blindness
  and of cancer of the tongue
  I can reassure you cancer of the tongue is not hereditary
  For gentlemen like your brother
  he said coarse cotton underwear is the right choice
  don't ever give him silk underwear
  believe me
  common coarse cotton underwear
  is best for him
  That loud repellent director's voice
  I hated it from the beginning
  but we have to put up with these people
  give useful hints of course

no matter how loathsome these people are
You would be well advised
to rub your brother down
at least once a week
with a Turkish towel
for six or seven minutes
and play part of the *Eroica* while you're doing it
As you know
Beethoven means something very special
to your brother
directly to her sister
and do you know
what else he said
quite expressly
don't ever give your brother the impression
that you are watching him
but don't ever let him out of your sight
It's not a bad idea
if we have guests now and then
invite some people I should think
parties are good for him
Ritter
To stay in London
and suffocate in London
for years he threatened us with that
I saved myself
I said to myself
it's my life
not his
and what if he had suffocated in London
or in Cambridge
or in Norway in his log cabin
You went to bring him back
not *me*
The continent will be the death of me
that's what he wrote so often on his postcards
Dene *goes into the kitchen*
Ritter *shouting after her*
A person who does not write manuscripts
but only *super*scriptions
lifelong logic
to herself
Nothing but blackmail
that's what he's always used against us

shouting
  I saved myself
  you became his slave
to herself
  To stay in London
  and to suffocate in London
shouting
  and then the Norwegian blackmail
  the so-called log cabin designed against himself
  Summer clothing fetishism
  that's what he accused me of
  spoiled my dancing lessons for me
  when I read Goethe
  he boxed my ears
  he spied on me in town
  called me a liar every chance he got
Dene
  You've always hated him
Ritter
  That's always been your calumny
Dene
  You've resented his every phrase
  You've always hated his way of thinking
  no matter what he did
  you hated it
Ritter
  His hatred of children
  has always scared me
Dene *coming out of the kitchen*
  I wonder
  if he deliberately didn't wear socks
  or whether he forgot to put them on
  do you know what else the director said
  I know you hate it when your brother uses suspenders
  please let him keep his suspenders
Ritter
  The doctors always think of everything
Dene
  The whole time he said
  Well-Tempered Clavier
  while I was signing the release
  I wonder whether Doctor Frege
  is the right doctor
  but he's the only one we have

Ritter
  To stay in London
  and suffocate in London
Dene
  On Sunday he wants to go to the *Musikverein*
  to the philharmonic concert
  do you know what they are playing
Ritter *shakes her head*
Dene
  Beethoven probably
  and Schönberg
  and Webern
  are you coming along
Ritter
  No
  I hate those concerts
  for years
  it's been the same pieces over and over again
  the same conductors
  the same people
Dene
  But with Ludwig
  it will be quite different
  The director says
  these concerts are indispensable
  therapeutic matinees so to speak
  we can't let him go by himself
  Why don't you come along once at least
  You haven't been to the *Musikverein* in such a long time
  We'll sit in Row Eight
  our subscription seats
Ritter
  I'm bored by those matinees
Dene
  But that is music
  that can be heard over and over again
Ritter
  Not by me it isn't
  it has all been heard
  ultimately it has all been heard
  and everything has been seen
Dene
  That's your megalomania

Ritter
Leave me in peace
Dene
I'm setting the table
and you sit there reading the paper
as though none of this were your affair
goes into the kitchen
Ritter *shouting after her*
Now you have your philosopher brother in the house
and you have to cope with him somehow
Dene
He's *your* brother as well
Ritter
Yes but *I* didn't take him out of Steinhof
Dene
But we had both discussed everything
together
Ritter
But *you* decided
to take him out of Steinhof
at your own risk
Dene
But don't you want him
home as well
he's your brother too
Ritter
Yes
Dene
If we are here
together for him
after all it's not the first time we've tried
There was nothing he wanted more
than to go to the *Musikverein*
on Sunday
Ritter
Beethoven
Brahms
that Schönberg always the same
that boring Webern
What there's too much of in Beethoven
there's too little of in Webern
I beg you
spare me

the philharmonic concerts
why don't you two take Doctor Frege with you
Dene
    While I was drawing a bath for him
he twice said *cryogenics philosophical*
he wanted to make a note of it straight away
so I ran to fetch his notepad
but when I got back
he screamed at me
that he had never said *cryogenics philosophical*
and had not asked for his notepad either
he insisted
that I stay in the bathroom
until he was completely naked
I was to tell him that he was ugly
you're not ugly you're beautiful
I said
and it wasn't a lie of course
and of course he really is beautiful
The keepers always enjoy looking at me
the doctors too
he said
bunch of perverts
they enjoy beating me too
and I enjoy being beaten by them
and my fellow patients he said
enjoy looking at me too
and enjoy beating me
But I never beat them
I never hit back he said
Naked Ludwig is a welcome sight he said
and immersed himself in the tub
I finally had to say three times
that he was ugly
after he had stood up quite straight in front of me
and I had to say it with a straight face
and I did say it with a straight face
and it really wasn't a laughing matter
Ritter
    Why three times
Dene
    I don't know
three times I had to say
you are ugly

I said it although I didn't want to
and while I did he touched
Ritter
What
Dene
Oh you always bring me to the point
where I admit everything
Ritter
Pervert
Dene
And you
Ritter
Your brother's prick
driving you almost to distraction
isn't that it
Dene *goes into the kitchen*
Ritter *shouting after her*
You do provoke him you know
into acting like that toward you
you are both bogged down in your infantilism
but that's your problem
and his problem
reading
A postcard
that was posted in Linz
in the year twenty-one
that's to say three years after the end of World War I
arrived in Vienna yesterday
shouting toward the kitchen
It's the bath water
you run the bath water
very hot bath water
and that drives him crazy
and you take advantage of him
that's what it is
you do it on purpose
reading
Gas explosion in the Third District
two housewives dead
mutilated beyond recognition
shouting into the kitchen
Our breakfasts
haven't changed in twenty years
not in thirty years

we've been spreading the same thing
on the same bread for thirty years
and we've been drinking the same tea with it
don't you think we should
do away with ourselves
for this reason alone
Two actresses from the Josefstadt Theatre
doing away with themselves
wouldn't that be a headline
shouting into the kitchen
Played the viola
yes you did that too
I played the piano
you the viola
because Uncle Friedrich played the viola
Had to
Ah well
throws the newspaper down, jumps up and goes into the kitchen
Dene *and* **Ritter** *enter with two large dishes and place them on
the table*
Ritter
I heated it up
Dene
Of course what else
Ritter
Heated it up yourself at any rate
Dene *goes into the kitchen*
Ritter *shouting after her as she is setting the table*
For twenty years
you've been transcribing his manuscripts
I'm convinced
that one day
they will even be printed
they'll be published by a major house
Logic I
Logic II
That will be to your credit
with the assistance of my sister etcetera
taking a taste from one of the dishes
Without you after all
there would *be* no manuscript by him
he thinks it out
and you type it
put it in order

even the spelling
you transcribe it
without you there wouldn't be a Ludwig any more
nothing of his
that's to your credit
one day he calls it art
then again
philosophy
or calls it nonsense
and when he dictates to you
he despises you
but you're happy enough to type it up
you are completely absorbed in his dictation
Our brother is a genius
not a fool
one day they'll be working on him
at all the universities
in America
everywhere
even though he himself
over and over again
calls everything he's ever written
nonsense
not senseless nonsense
The Steinhof sojourns
are his summer vacations
instead of going to Sils-Maria with us
he goes to Steinhof
taking a taste from one of the dishes
instead of going to Lucerne with us
he goes to Steinhof
Not even a Christmas with us
our holiday hater
sings in the choir at Steinhof on Christmas Eve
in his institutional clothes
father told him
that he wouldn't be any good even in the acting business
that was the most scathing indictment
When people ask him about his relatives
he says my sisters are actresses
at the Josefstadt
not without talent
my father died of cancer of the tongue
Dene *comes out of the kitchen*

Ritter
The acting business
that's all that was left for us
nothing more
I never wanted a profession
and you
Dene
I don't know
Ritter
You had stage presence
Dene
Yes perhaps
Ritter
In comedies
and tragedies
Dene
Just because our uncle
was a theatre manager
Ritter
The daughters of Worringer the industrial tycoon
fled to their theatre manager uncle
because they were bored
had had enough of life
ended up in the Josefstadt theatre
Dene
If you say so
Ritter
He always called you the gifted one
the one for whom there was hope
I was always the untalented one
for whom there was no hope
Because he loved us our uncle
Genteel daughters of genteel ladies
in insipid plays
with background music
And because our brother hated it
we joined the theatre
that was a decisive factor
because our brother hated the theatre
and because our parents hated the theatre
hatred of the theatre was the greatest in our family
Dene
Perhaps

Ritter

  And Ludwig took the philosophical route
  suicidal
  a lone-wolf suicidal
  Logic I
  Logic II
  written alternately in London and Norway
  typed up by his sister
  his eccentric magnum opus
  by his older sister of course
  The precision instrument
  as he calls you
  that's what you've been for twenty years
  If you play the piano
  you cannot type
  that was my good fortune
  but typing and playing the viola
  that's all right

Dene

  It's always your unhappiness which speaks out

Ritter *scornfully*

  And in your case it's just your happiness

Dene *sitting down at the table and looking it over*

  I want to set the table for him
  just as he loves it
  just as mother used to set it
  just as father loved it
straightens up the cutlery

Ritter

  Geometrimania even on the dining table
  exercises in submissiveness

Dene *looking at the clock*

  After all it's only a try

Ritter

  The eighteenth
  or the nineteenth

Dene

  If Anna had done the cooking
  it would be better of course
  but we would have had to put up with her
  this way we're alone
  undisturbed
  just the three of us the first time for a long while

The first evening is the most difficult of all
No candles
he hates candles on the table
hatred of illumination
He always liked clear soups

Ritter

With his shoes on his bare feet
and reciting the Schopenhauer sentence
and three times you had to say
that he was ugly

Dene

Over and over again the word antipathy
while I was walking back to the car with him

Ritter

Ludwig is a fanatic about cleanliness
pathological naturally
like our father
but father didn't carry it to such extremes
and father didn't end up in Steinhof
Worringer the industrial tycoon
who used to wash his hands
thirty times a day
and nobody knew about it
except us

sits down at the table

Dene

Transcribed the so-called dualism chapter
last night
not a wink
only wondering
how shall I bring him home
on the phone with the director twice
And don't forget
two tablets three times a day
not three twice
that was already enough to drive me crazy
the way the director continually said *intelligent* man
Your philosopher brother
is over the worst he said
but remember
that he'll be vulnerable all his life

Ritter

In Zurich it was nice

do you remember
free and easy
Dene
He only dictates what he's thought *out*
Our anti-Kant
It answers a need in him
to dictate to me
it's all therapeutic the director said
That's the death penalty I pronounce on you
said Ludwig my dictating to you
or at least and in any case a life sentence
even worse
always on the brink of insanity
but never going over the brink
but always on the brink of insanity
if we leave that border region
we are dead
Ritter
Going to Rome now
you don't need me after all
you are the really important person in his life
not me
I'm just a burden
I'm the one who makes him nervous
I can't even cook
I can't even heat things up
looking round the room
Everything still
the way our parents furnished it
nothing's been changed
since our parents died
I would have cleared everything out
everything
but you objected
now you're almost suffocating here
Dene
But you could have gone away
to Rome for example
or to Amsterdam
I wouldn't have put any obstacles in your path
but then you'd forfeit your contract
Ritter
Didn't go away

that's it
but not for Ludwig's sake like you
because I couldn't
because you've always paralyzed me
kept me chained up
and not because of the Josefstadt either

Dene

I kept you chained
You are completely independent
you've always been free to do
what you liked
but you didn't *want* to go away
You blame me you've always blamed me
for chaining you to this house
but you could have gone at any time
wherever you liked

Ritter

True

Dene

I've often said go
you didn't go
I was never interested in men
but you were
and yet you stayed

Ritter

Not for Ludwig's sake

Dene

Ludwig Ludwig
I'm here for Ludwig
but not you
you stayed
because you didn't want to take any risks
because of your Josefstadt connection
that's the truth

Ritter

Your truth

Dene

My truth

Ritter

Ludwig means everything to me
that's what you've always said
Now you've got him back in your gilded cage

Dene *rising*

And you
Ritter
My favorite brother
my favorite philosopher
that's what you've always said
Dene *on her way to the kitchen*
My favorite brother
my favorite philosopher
Ritter
Your anti-Kant
picks up the newspaper from the floor
Dene
You've never done more than put up with Ludwig
never really looked after him
but then you are the younger sister
Why are you always talking about Rome
and Paris
and you don't go
I've only ever known you to lie in bed
eating what Anna has cooked
reading the paper
and forever disappointed in love
Ritter
After mother's death
you started talking the way *she* always talked
to this day
adopted her way of walking
and you even tug at your hair
like mother
and you have the same way of saying *supper*
and then you sit there and say nothing just like mother
and you also say Ludwig like her
every time I hear you say Ludwig
I can hear mother saying *Ludwig*
To Rome next week
rising and going to the window
or to Normandy
or the Shakespeare in the Josefstadt after all
just as long as it gets me out of here
Dene
And in a just a few days
you'll be back again
that's your misfortune you know

Ritter
>You're quite right there
>you're my clairvoyant

Dene
>You have always directed everything
>to your misfortune
>Your brother is right
>you attract it
>your misfortune I mean
>There are those who attract it
>there are those who repel it

Ritter *reading*
>I always felt
>as if you two
>were going behind my back
>In our elementary school
>you were five years ahead of me
>my whole life
>but both of us are unhappy
>you have your unhappiness
>I have mine
>you cook
>when you have no alternative
>I read the papers
>newspaper addiction
>for which you blame me
>I never blame you for anything
>myself yes
>but not you
>To Budapest with Ludwig
>without saying a word
>I didn't blame you
>to *The Magic Flute* with Ludwig
>all behind my back
>no blame from me
>I always swallowed it all
>as they say
>I was always watching everything
>you've straightened everything out
>I don't know
>who suffered more
>Disease is a sacred process
>religion he said

you think I don't see
what you are to him
Dene
We shall never find a way out of
our errors
Ritter
Bought five shirts
the most expensive
and took them out to Steinhof
and he didn't wear a single one of them
gave them all away
after all
it's my money too
our money
Refractoriness
he explained it to me
the last time I visited him
snow falling outside the window
he said then that he was going blind rapidly
complained as usual that there were bugs
that the door to the terrace was stuck
that the windows wouldn't close
Dene
I'll phone that Doctor Frege
Seven hundred schillings for ten minutes
there's doctors for you
we ask them to suggest a way to help
but they make no suggestions they don't help
But Doctor Frege
has known him the longest
an experienced doctor so to speak
as far as Ludwig is concerned
Ritter
He keeps looking for sympathy
but of course he offends everybody
he antagonizes everybody
Dene
Indifference to philosophy on your part
he got back to that again
the stupid sister
that's what you are
I'm the officious one
witless both of us

coming from the kitchen with a dish
    He needs *me*
    I'm the one he depends on
    not on *you*
    but you're the one he loves
Ritter *bursting out laughing*
    Me
    it's you he loves
    you
    the useful one
    I'm the useless one
    whom he hates
Dene *wipes each piece of cutlery with a napkin*
Ritter
    You're the one he's always favored
    first favored
    then loved
    you are the one who's closest to him
    Cutlery china
    everything has to be perfect
holding up a fork to the light and inspecting it
    he sees everything
    and we're afraid
    that he might see something
    that he shouldn't
placing the fork on the table and taking a spoon, holds it up to the
    light and inspects it
    Even as a child
    a horror of dirty cutlery
    Always a fresh napkin
    and most demanding when it came to food
placing the spoon on the table
    A fresh shirt three times a day
    Fresh bed linen every other day
    Our parents
    invested everything in him
    he was their child
    what were we
Ritter *reading*
    We were conceived by
    Henry James
    we were not their children
Dene
    That's what father always said

in his need to inflict pain
and Ludwig says it too
father thought just the way Ludwig does
Ritter
One was the industrial tycoon
the other the philosophical tycoon
Dene
Oh nonsense (*sitting*)
Ludwig is so infirm
and so frail
Ritter
That's what *you* think
that's how *you* see him
because that's how you want to see Ludwig
because that's how you *have* to see him
these people appear so infirm
but they're stronger than anyone
Dene
But I know but I can see
how helpless he is
Ritter
He has you in his power
totally
Ludwig is a brute
that's the truth
and you know it too
a thug with philosophical intentions
but you just can't admit that to yourself
that would screw up your whole concept
reading aloud
Never before
have so many Italians
come to Vienna
inundating the city
Everything Austrian
fascinates the Italians
Austrian history
Austrian art
everything Austrian
Dene
If it weren't for Ludwig we wouldn't
be here at all
looking round
we wouldn't be here any longer

everything would have been sold
you perhaps would be in Rome
who knows where I would be
Ludwig holds us together

Ritter

He ruined us long ago
and annihilated us

Dene

But you don't even believe that yourself
you won't tell him that to his face
and anyway it's a lie

Ritter

Insofar as truth
is also just a lie
everything is a lie
according to Ludwig
a lie and a falsehood

*throwing the newspaper away and jumping up and going to
    the window*
speaking directly to her sister

Ludwig is your property
and vice versa
Ludwig owns you
and I am condemned
to keep looking at this depravity
Oh how everything gets on my nerves in this place
You are the most ruthless person
unscrupulously ruthless

looking out of the window

But Rome would be just as unbearable
Because we've already seen everything
Where does our brother get the right
to possess us

with sudden intensity

The Josefstadt is my salvation
I will act again   ˙
it doesn't matter what I play
Whatever *you* can do
I can do also
Turn one's back on the theatre
that was just insincere posturing
for the sake of a philosophical thug

turning round speaking directly to her sister

We must be on our guard
against him
he's intent on
ruining us completely
for years
for decades he's been doing his work of destruction
We are the ones who need help
not him
we are the victims
not him
it's *ourselves* we must help
not him
going up to her sister
Our mental cripple
is destroying us
has almost succeeded in destroying us
that's his triumph
that's his doing
Dene
You're getting worked up
when sober reflection alone
is appropriate
you've plunged headlong
into your Ludwig complex
Ritter
That's what *he* said
didn't he
not you
Dene
Even if he did say it
you do have a Ludwig complex
If only you could finally realize
that this cul-de-sac
is the only possible existence for us
but you're not ready to do that
and besides you are still too young
Ritter
To have swallowed
the logician's bait
that's what so repellent
Dene *inspects a knife*
Ritter
A soothing atmosphere

secure and warm
that's what our father always said
Ludwig has often repeated
that phrase
mocking father
that phrase has become
more and more absurd
with the passage of time
By and by
this house has become
a hell for us
The Worringer hell
that's how Ludwig himself has often referred to it
directly to her sister
But really can't you see that
we have in fact turned this house
into a Worringer hell
and not even innocently
we have quite consciously made this house
into this Worringer hell
It's just that *you* won't admit
who is the devil in that hell

Dene
After the soup a slice of melon
I don't think that's wrong
I don't think that's wrong
perhaps you should refrain
from drinking wine
if he sees
that you're drinking wine

Ritter
All right
I'll restrain myself
but just this once
just this one first time
It would be better
if Anna were here
as it is you'll spend the whole time
running between the kitchen and the dining room
he does hate that so much
he's always hated that
housewives constantly running
from the dining room to the kitchen
maddening

Dene

> You've never liked me
> even as a very small child
> you hated me
> He likes clear soup
> he hates so-called thick soup

Ritter

> At first it was our parents
> who spoon-fed him
> then we did
> it's sickening
> the way you constantly
> spoon-feed him
> It was always said that he was
> our little weakling
> until he turned into that monster
> the little helpless child turned into
> that megalomaniac
> that philosopher
> Beware of the weak
> our father always used to say
> for they are in fact the strong
> the weak rule us
> not the strong
> the so-called rules us
> not the actual the real the factual

going to the clock and winding it

> We are constantly shying away
> from everything
> he doesn't shy away from anything
> he only cares about thinking
> but who's to say
> that his thinking amounts to anything
> perhaps what he thinks is all mere nonsense
> perhaps he's just thought nonsense till now
> since he really is mad after all
> since in fact he calls Steinhof
> his real home
> My Ludwig you say
> and you think
> my Ludwig my philosopher
> when in reality he is only your fool
> your favorite fool

the brother as the favorite fool
as the favorite perversity
Dene
There's nothing to say to that
Ritter
That's your strong suit
that's what you have in common with Ludwig
to say nothing
when there is everything to be said
not to respond
when everything has been asked
You two will soon have smothered me completely
with your hypocrisy
Dene *goes into the kitchen*
Ritter *shouting after her*
You're stirring the soup around
and all you're thinking about
is how best to torture me
and our brother is amusing himself
at our stupidity
sitting down at the table and shouting into the kitchen
he philosophizes
in order to destroy me
and for the same reason
you're stirring the soup around
Dene *coming out of the kitchen with a bread basket*
For thirty years
the same argument
placing the bread basket on the table
Just the way our father
used to argue with our uncle
but then it wasn't about Ludwig
but about the factory
it was just as odious
after a pause
I imagined this evening would be
so beautiful
After months for the first time
to be dining again together with Ludwig
just the three of us
undisturbed
Ritter
Sibling affection

a threesome
rising to straighten a picture on the wall and sitting down again
    You have always planned
    everything in your head
    and tried with all the means in your power
    to put your plans into action
    without regard for others
    You took Ludwig out of the institution
    you sent Anna away
    you decided who was to sit where at this table
    it's always *you* that's done everything
Dene *sits down at the table*
Ritter
    And Ludwig doesn't even know
    that he owes everything he is
    to you
    You decided to take up the typewriter
    I the piano
    as a second artistic activity
    Developed a taste for it
    that's it
    You transcribe what he has thought *out*
    At the very height of craziness
    you type out
    what he has thought out
    and I play the piano while you do it
    improvising philosophically so to speak
    at the piano
Dene
    I took four pairs of shoes to Steinhof
    in two weeks
    and he gave them all away
Ritter
    Humanitarian megalomania
Dene
    You're against anything
    and everything
    that's your misfortune
Ritter
    But our brother
    is our genius
    domiciled to be sure in Steinhof
    but matter for discussion

at English universities
achieved the status of a topic for dissertations in philosophy
more thoughtfully
Refuge in the theatre
didn't do us any good
playacting nothing more
Utensils
that's what he calls us
you who protect him
screen him so to speak
a utensil
and he abuses us
laughing
you
who type up his thinking
who reproduce him so sedulously
sacrifices her nights
for his thoughts

Dene
Bought five shirts for him
and then I meet all those people wearing them
The director had Ludwig's hat on
while he was talking to me
your brother you know
presented me with his hat
then I had to put it on
a bet you know
I bet your brother
that I would keep his hat on my head
while you were in my office
I cannot tell you what the stakes were
but as you can see
I am in the process
of winning the bet
Don't think madam
that I am crazy
said the director
of course everyone says
that all directors of madhouses are crazy
the directors are crazier than the patients entrusted to their care
that's what people say
because that's what they like to hear
No no a bet
nothing more

Furthermore the director said
your brother has completed the Kierkegaard chapter
which he'd been working on for eight months
Steinhof the philosopher's retreat he said
several times
Steinhof the philosopher's retreat
Your brother will be very famous one day
and then people will say
here in Steinhof
is where his work was born
and we hope that then they will also say
that here in Steinhof he completed it
That odious voice you know it very well
My hand shook as I signed
It's your responsibility of course
the director said
Suddenly Ludwig was there
and said
you've won the bet director
Ludwig took the hat off the director's head
and put it on
This hat
is much too small for me said Ludwig
took the hat off again
and put it back on the director's head
You've won the bet
my respects to you Ludwig said
then he wrote out a check
and put that check in the director's
coat pocket
Ritter
And then what happened
Dene
Nothing
I said come along Ludwig
let's go
let's leave this place quickly
The director accompanied me out of the door
Ludwig had gone on ahead
Ritter *inquiringly*
And then
Dene
He blew kisses
to the people

who were standing around everywhere
because it was visiting hours you know
and then he proceeded to put his hand into his coat pocket
and pull out a bundle of hundred schilling bills
and started waving it about
and suddenly he distributed the whole bundle
bill by bill among the people
Patients and visitors were fighting over the hundred schilling bills
Ritter
And you did nothing to stop him
Dene
No
I wanted to take him out of the institution
without a struggle
he was quite calm
now and again someone would call to him
by his first name
Ludwig
and time and again he would blow kisses to them all
Dualism that's what it is
that's what it is
he exclaimed several times
catafalquism
militarism
he got wrapped up in these words
then suddenly he embraced me and said
how happy I am
that you are here
Ritter *getting up and going to the window, looking out*
You went to fetch him
not me
he can't accuse me
of fetching him away
Wasn't that
what you were after
in wanting me to come along with you to fetch him
a sort of complicity
when he realizes
that it was a mistake
to take him out
at this juncture
Dene *picking up a knife and holding it up to the light*
Ritter
Complicity

that's what you wanted
that's why you suggested early this morning
that I should come along
with you to fetch him
no no
I didn't fetch him
you fetched him
Dene
Why do you always assume
only the worst
Whatever I do
has in your eyes
an ulterior motive
your life is one long need
to be suspicious
Ritter
You do nothing
without a reason
Dene
The older one
is responsible for everything
that's it
you've been using that argument against me
for as long as I can remember
No no
Ludwig got into the car quite calmly
the director was still bowing
when we were already
more than a hundred meters away
Was he sure that he had packed everything
and taken everything with him
I asked Ludwig
by then we were already driving along Hill Road
yes he said
everything
Ritter *suddenly curious*
What sort of part
is the blind woman
a big part
Dene
Only one short appearance
two sentences that's all
Ritter
And you subject yourself to that

Dene
　After all I haven't acted
　for four years
　but this interests me
　fascinates me
　and besides it won't wear me out completely
Ritter
　Two sentences
　spoken by a blind woman
Dene
　I'm not worried
　about playing a big part
　I could have if I'd wanted to
　no no two sentences
　but how
Ritter
　You were always ambitious
　on the stage
　you never took chances
Dene
　Every chance my dear every chance
Ritter
　Yes every chance
Dene
　The many walk-on parts
　I've played
　when I could have played
　the very biggest
　It's not a question of how long
　an actor is on the stage
　it's merely a question of *how*
　two or three minutes of brilliant theatre
Ritter
　Of course of course
Dene
　Our views
　were always not only different
　always opposed
　You always only wanted to play big parts
　I never did
　The difference is
　that because of Ludwig
　I didn't act for four years

not like you
because I didn't get a big part
I could have played a big part at any time
Ludwig made it impossible
Ritter
In any event
a sacrifice to Ludwig
Dene
As you see it
Ritter
Your talent is the greater of the two
your talent is the opposite of mine
You're a born histrionic
I don't mean that in a pejorative sense
on the contrary
you're an actress through and through
I have to give my all every time   ~
everything comes easily to you
because to the genius everything comes easily
Dene *bursting out laughing*
The genius
An actor is never a genius
interpreters are not geniuses
least of all actors
And nothing I've ever done has come easily
that's where you're wrong
I know that I can be good for only three minutes
and so I only appear for three minutes
I was never ambitious to do
a whole play a so-called big part
Dene
But you also played big parts well
even the ones where you're on all the time so to speak
it didn't matter what
it was always good
no one could have acted those parts like you
no question of that
Dene
Whatever is going on inside my sister I wonder
to make her so unhappy
she has everything
everything a person can have
and is unhappy

rising and fetching the large lamp so that she can place it in the
    middle of the table, taking a step backwards so that she can look
    at the lamp
    No
    no no
    how tasteless that lamp is
    I've never noticed it
    an extremely tasteless lamp
picking the lamp up again and putting it back into the place she had
    taken it from, going to the window and looking out
    I'm not really an actress at all
    I just wanted to be among people
    that was the reason
    possibly I did have a modest talent for it
    an urge to playact probably
    you've always had that too
    but not professionally
    anything professional has always put me off
    only because I didn't want to isolate myself
    that's the truth
    just to be allowed to attend rehearsals
    when I was in acting school
    was my salvation you know
    not actual interest in the art of acting
Ritter *has risen*
Dene
    No certainly not
    To be together with people of our own age
looking her sister in the face
    And of course the fact
    that our uncle had shares in the Josefstadt
    and was also manager of the theatre
    played a part
    without him I would not
    have taken up acting later on
    They need a girl in the Shakespeare
    you're it my child
    that was all
    the rest is history
going to the mirror and looking into it
    You're quite a different case
    a real actress quite consciously
    with the highest aspirations
turning round

You are much better than I am you know
but in the end fortune was always on my side
that's what it is nothing else
specious good fortune
Our rivalry in the theatre
I never took it seriously
when you acted well
I was always pleased
looking at the clock, then
   It's time
   he came
going out and calling as loudly as she can
   Ludwig

CURTAIN

Dinner

The doors to the kitchen are now on the left
Ritter *and* **Voss** *at the table eating and drinking*
Voss is seated opposite the portrait of his father, he is drinking water,
   Ritter is drinking white wine
Voss *leaning forward*
   Walking tall
   do you know what that means
   all the time till now I couldn't
   suddenly walking tall again
sitting up straight
   According to regulations
leaning forward and whispering
   She brought me the wrong paper
   and made it impossible
   for me to write down chapter six
   everything lost put the kibosh on everything
   I had told her the paper
   on which I wrote Logic I
   but she wasn't listening
sitting up straight
   Flying the kite in Glossop
   do you remember
   the time in England a nice time

Then he went to England
and studied mathematics
said the director
Of course I heard everything
that he said
it isn't the Norwegian problem
it's the Cambridge problem said the director
Time and again *from a wealthy family* he said
and *volunteered for the army*
Then mathematics got the upper hand
for what is philosophy if not mathematics
mathematics on the brink
leaning forward
Once I drew him the propeller blade that I had constructed
on a piece of official stationery
he was astonished
I *don't* want a single room I said
please *not* a single room
and then wouldn't you know
a single room
a single room if you please
It isn't the log cabin problem he said
it's the Cambridge problem
The rich simply have
the most difficulties of any
he said
leaning forward
Our sister confided to him
that at eighteen
looking round
I slept with our mother
She said it without any trace of embarrassment
that amused the director
I would not have said that
tattletale
sitting up
He first experimented with kites and balloons
and then he turned to propulsion motors
she said
she thought that I was in my room
while all the time I was in the director's outer office
and was waiting for her
which she had no way of knowing
She and the director were discussing a trip to Madrid

a trip she wants to take
on her own
If you had paid attention
to what I was saying
everything would not now be lost to me
I said to her
you have destroyed everything of mine
I can't make any notes on *this* paper
Irritation ensued
she left me at once
I saw how she hated me
she hated everything as she went away
she even persecuted my fellow sufferers
with her hatred
I did not read the newspapers
which she had brought along for me
I distributed them
I should not have done that
for then they all started dancing beside themselves
with the fun of playing with the papers
She thinks she types without making any mistakes
she makes nothing but mistakes
and yet there is nothing easier
than typing from a neat manuscript
She says she's returning to the stage
she's going to act again
Ritter
    Yes
Voss *leaning forward and whispering*
    A comedy isn't it
Ritter *nods*
Voss
    Sisters actresses
    theatre birds
    stage twitter
laughing
leaning forward and whispering
    My idea was
    to go further
    than all the others
    beyond all the others
sitting up
    We are chained to oddities
    Do you understand me

to oddities
and suffocate in monotony
Dene *enters with a large meat plate and sits down*
Ritter *to her*
Do you remember Glossop
Dene
Yes of course
Ritter
How little has happened to us since then
Dene
For heaven's sake
Ritter
Ludwig says
that you brought him the wrong paper
and that made him lose a lot of time
Dene *serves out pieces of meat*
Ritter
How long has it been
since Glossop
Dene
Twenty-two years
I know exactly
my greatest disappointment
Ritter
Speak for yourself
I was happy in Glossop
Dene
I read a biography of Mozart
I was in bed the whole time
with a sore throat
while you and Ludwig
were experimenting with the kite
Voss
My kite experiment
my definitive discovery
But I discovered something entirely different
from what I thought I had
Years later I knew
that in Glossop I had discovered
something quite different
Ritter
I had a decisive share
in that discovery

Voss

Of course

Dene

I was terribly ill

Ritter

You didn't want to go to Glossop
you got ill in Glossop
because you didn't want to go to Glossop
you ran a fever on the very first day

Voss

Glossop had a decisive influence on me

Dene

Yes you regenerated yourselves in Glossop
But I love
biographies of artists
that was my advantage
My sore throat was only half as bad with Mozart there
rises and goes out

Ritter

She's playing a blind woman
short role
on the stage for two perhaps three minutes
perhaps she'll taste blood
I'm sure
it will do her good
What a good thing that we never completely broke off
our connections
with theatre people
as far as I'm concerned
I've always cultivated contacts
with theatre people
but I'm not ready to take
just any part
but even if we don't perform
we must keep in shape
I work at my art every day you understand

Voss

Two artists for sisters
I don't know
has that brought me good luck
or bad
more bad luck than good
certainly more bad luck

Ritter
My Ludwig
the way he thinks
our egoist
Wouldn't you like another slice of melon
Voss *leaning forward and whispering*
She brought me five shirts
and I gave them all away
of course that annoyed her
but it's my money after all
The philosopher gives his thoughts away
it is his thinking after all
sitting up straight and taking a slice of melon
In Skjolden I thought
I can't go on
The director said
that was my Norwegian problem
the log cabin idyll
In the evening before going to bed
we have inspection
and the doctor insists
that we answer our names
He says good night
then we say good night
the light is put out automatically
Dene *enters with a bowl of salad and sits down*
Voss
Put out automatically
Not bad food
in the institution
Everyone may eat as much as he wants
the problem is
that I have no one to converse with in the night
for they all sleep soundly
The nights in Steinhof are absolutely quiet
Dene
Now you're at home
and you can do what you want
putting a piece of meat on Ludwig's plate
Now everything
connected with Steinhof is over
forget it
would you like to hear some music perhaps

Voss
  No
Dene
  I've bought a new *Ninth*
Voss *inquiringly*
  Yes
  Walking *tall*
  do you know what that means
Dene
  The afternoon walk
  will do you good
  or whatever you like
  Perhaps you want to read
  make some music perhaps
  or we'll invite company
Ritter
  What company
Dene
  Company
  people
directly to Ludwig
  Who would you like to see
  Perhaps it's better if we don't
  invite people right away
  perhaps it's best if you simply sleep as long as you want to
  Rest
  rest rest rest
starting to serve meat but the others do not want any more meat
directly to Ludwig
  Or do you want to dictate to me
  in the afternoon
  I spent the whole night with you
  with the chapter on dualism
  to be quite honest
  I don't understand any of it
Ritter *to Dene*
  Is the front gate locked
Dene
  Of course
rises and goes out
Ritter *calling after her*
  There's a draft
  be sure to close the kitchen door

to Voss
> That's right isn't it
> there *is* a draft
> I'm so susceptible to drafts

Dene *closes the kitchen door*

Ritter
> *She's* the one who's sick
> not you
> *she's* one who's sick
> It's good that you're here
> we were on the point of suffocating
> each other
> Our sister suffers
> from paranoia
> between you and me
> she tyrannizes Anna
> daft about cleanliness
> not a moment's peace
> paces up and down in her room
> rushes into mine and asks
> whether I have an earache *too*
> I ask her why I should have an earache
> then she says
> because *I* have an earache
> a terrible earache
> I can't sleep all night
> because she's always running up and down
> in her room
> When I go into her room
> she'll be sitting in front of her jewel box
> shoves her bed with her own hands
> first into one corner
> then into the other
> Two water-diviners were there
> they kept putting your bed
> into a different place
> now it's back in the place
> where it always was
> she thinks she's alone
> and brushes your clothes
> for hours on end
> while I'm there all the time
> watching her

she opens all the drawers in your room
takes everything out
wipes out all the drawers
whispering
when I went into her room
last week
she had your dress trousers on
frightened to death she said
she didn't know
what had made her
put on your dress trousers
asking
Meat
whispering
She sits at the window without a stitch on
and spoons up her yoghurt
as she listens to the Schumann
piano concerto
Voss
I don't want any more meat
Ritter
I don't know
what she'll do in Madrid
she's never said anything
relating to Madrid
whispering
She has a cactus
in her room
a thirty-year-old cactus
Dene *enters*
Ritter
Please close the door
Dene *closes the kitchen door and sits down at the table, stands up
again at once and clears the china away in order to put it on the
sideboard, sits down again*
Ritter
Ludwig looks well
as though he'd just come back from vacation
Dene
He does
Ritter
He doesn't look a bit
like a philosopher

Voss
But what does a philosopher
look like
Dene
Like you
since you *are* a philosopher
Voss
Philosopher philosopher
anti-artist
Ritter
Just come back from vacation
While we were sweltering in this humidity
almost suffocating
our Ludwig was on vacation
Dene *to Voss*
I got the right paper for you
A thousand sheets
a whole packet
on your desk
I brushed your clothes
pressed your trousers
everything freshly laundered
No more Steinhof smell
Voss
No more Steinhof smell
Dene *looking through the window*
And if it rains in the afternoon
then it is most pleasant
not to have the feeling
that you have to do anything
Voss
Read a bit
when the sky begins to darken
draw the curtains
read
Dene
That's not something I bother about
when there's so much to do
and everything falls to me
more or less
Ritter
A matinee
which was always our salvation as children
is now out of the question

afternoon tea at Aunt Margaret's
how easy it was then
to escape from despair
a cup of cocoa
and the map on the floor
that's no longer enough
Soon it won't even be enough
to take a biography to bed with you
Dene
Music is very often a salvation
Ritter
You're right
but soon we'll not even be able to bear listening to music
when suddenly and then for ever
our ears hate music
because we misuse it
in order to survive so to speak
Voss
Thinking is quite undisturbed
by that
however much we misuse it
it is always possible
after a while everything begins to get on our nerves
not thinking
the person who thinks
can grow old with impunity
Or have a crazy idea
all your life
a single crazy idea
Listening reading looking that's all nothing
compared with this one single crazy idea
but that is my problem
Dene *rises and goes out carrying a few plates with her*
Voss
A mathematical solution naturally
solved absolutely mathematically
How miserable I feel sometimes
just like a dying man
then suddenly everything's all right again
because I think
that I shall overcome everything just
by thinking
not by being thoughtful
by thinking

whispering
　　I didn't intend
　　to come here
　　My sisters are my destroyers
　　they annihilate me
　　that's what I always tell myself
　　I said to the director
　　when my sister comes
　　tell her
　　that I don't want to go home
　　if I go home
　　it will be the death of me
　　family means death
　　and I have no friends
　　if I disregard the fact
　　that my fellow patients are my friends
　　But she was relentless
　　I didn't want to run the risk of
　　quarreling with her
　　lack of comprehension is the one bond
　　between myself and my sisters
　　that's what I thought
　　you do understand me don't you
　　you've always understood me better
　　than your sister
　　she has always only understood herself
　　But I shall only stay home for a very very short time
　　I said to the director
leaning right forward
　　Two three days
　　I'd be dead on the fourth you know
Dene *enters and sits*
　　There was a swallow
　　in the kitchen
　　hurt itself on the window
　　That Anna only makes a mess
　　I pay her the highest wages
　　and she only makes a mess
　　nothing is in its proper place
　　everything's dirty
　　the tragedy is
　　that we are at the mercy of these people
　　they exploit us blackmail us
　　slander us into the bargain

they drag us down into the dirt
wherever they can
treachery from below
is vile
Father was right
Write a letter to Ireland
this afternoon
it's long overdue
I'll write and tell them
not to come
what do they want here
we haven't seen them for twenty years
and just now of all times
I never could stand
our Irish relatives
a very polite letter of refusal
the afternoon will be ideal for that
serving potatoes, rice, and salad
    I said to the director
    that I knew
    how to deal with a philosopher
    gently I said
    at which he laughed
Voss
    Laughed
Ritter
    I'll start acting again in the autumn
    Shakespeare
    that's the plan
Voss
    My sisters are actresses
    I told the director
    when I saw him for the first time
    be careful
    they're stinking rich
    and are actresses
    That was all I needed I said
    for my sisters to be
    slaves of the theatre
    not without talent I said
    but I hate the theatre
    there is nothing I find more odious
    but the fact is
    that we have to make the best

of what we find the most odious
Don't think I'm going to
commit suicide
which is what my relatives are afraid of
it's an idea of course
but I demand a natural death
whatever that may be
I shan't do away with myself
never fear
So even during my first stay
they let me keep my suspenders
As you see
I said to the director this very morning
I have not done away with myself
You've known me these twenty years
and to this day I haven't done away with myself
Death after all comes to us of itself
when we want it
I said to the director
we don't have to use force

Dene
Here's a lovely piece of meat Ludwig
perhaps you still have room for it

Voss *refusing*
We have our terminal disease
and know
that we shall die of it
we can hasten this process of dying
hold it up drag it out
if we want to
but of course we know
that all that is just a matter of a short space of time
and we say to ourselves
at least let us pursue this thought a bit further
throw that one away
write this line down
complete the chapter
that's what gives us our greatest pleasure
that's why we go on existing
for no other reason
for except that we think
and cling to what we think
as far as we can

nothing is of interest to us anymore
I mean *my* thinking
and I
Dene *puts another piece of meat on his plate and pours gravy over it*
Voss
We certainly didn't go to England
for a pleasure trip
but because we wanted to invigorate
our thinking
to replace something stale with something completely new
I didn't go to Cambridge
to get my English Ph.D.
not for such a trifle
but because I saw a chance there
of thinking further
than I had been able to up to that point
All ties to relatives etcetera broken off
for that purpose alone
We cannot think
when we are tied to people and their needs
That does not mean
that people do not interest us
on the contrary
because everything we've done
has been directed at them with the greatest intensity
we have to free ourselves from them
Always sought simplicity
but never found it
nothing but the process of our dying
which makes us possible
We strive our whole lives just
for two or three pages of immortal writing
we want no more
but it is the highest goal all the same
The director did not understand
what I said
the director's way of thinking
isn't my way of thinking
he isn't willing
to think my thinking
although it would be possible
for him to think my thinking
But I only have the director in Steinhof

the patients are complete dullards
that's what's so fascinating
that they are such complete dullards
sitting up straight
At last walking tall again
do you two know what that means
Dene *pours gravy over the meat, which Voss has scarcely touched*
Voss
It's only when we are sick
that we are happy
looking round
I thought
that everything would be different
but you haven't altered it
Everything will be different I thought
Cling to everything
that's characteristic of you
It can only be a short visit
Dene
What are you saying
Voss
Only a short visit
The inferiority of life
we become quite conscious of it
when we return to a house like this
which we have left forever
Dene *has been trying to touch him with her hand but he has resisted*
Voss
We're going back
we're going back
don't you understand
It's all right to let my sister think
that I'm going back home
I have no intention
so I said to the director
of turning my back on Steinhof
this is my home nowhere else I said
My room is always at my disposal
I've got used to Steinhof
I shall die in Steinhof
not here
there is nothing more repellent
than dying in one's parents' house

you two may do that
it suits you
it doesn't suit me
For one moment I thought
it would be nice
just for a moment
We are always searching for the right path
and are always on it already
Perhaps I am crazy
it's possible
Dene
Made it specially for you Ludwig
your favorite gravy
Ritter
For heaven's sake leave him in peace
Dene *as the only one continuously and hastily eating*
I put myself out
but it's not appreciated
Voss
You know it's nothing more
than a process of atrophy
irresistible existence
to escape from boredom
but success is impossible
boredom
which is interrupted only
by fear of death
being irrevocably alone
I thought
but it was no use
crawled away to a hole in Norway
for the sake of an inadmissibility
cooped up in a wooden hut
with an idea
without success
destroyed everything in the end
years of chastisement
years of discipline
everything burned in a single moment
In Norway too
they refused me entrance
to the inn
one glance sufficed to turn me away

I thought
anyone as undemanding as I
cannot gain admittance
We have millions in our trousers pocket
and cannot do anything with them
hastily eating a few pieces
Thinking things over is not stimulating
but nauseating
that's what's bad about it
but it only has value
when it's nauseating
nauseating people
valuable people
We have tried everything
and at the end
we are always left on our own
to his older sister
Desserts were always
your forte
Veal beef pork
always ended up
in a disaster of frying oil and batter
Mother couldn't cook
she detested the kitchen
But since you're helping out with the cooking and
Ritter
She only heated the food up
Voss
and heated the food up
it's not half bad
Dene
I didn't want
Anna to be here
when you came home
Voss
Came home came home
This isn't my home
suddenly in a very low voice
When we submit to surgery
our lives can under certain circumstances
be lengthened
but I don't want that
Probability is something I hate
Dene *tries to put gravy onto his plate, but he refuses it*

Voss
   We really do
   enter into a contract
   but we break it
   every contract has to be broken
   When we've signed a contract
   we have to break it
   Contracts are fatal
for a long time now he has been repeatedly looking at the portrait of
   his father on the wall facing him
   Either we don't sign one
   or if we have signed one
   it has to be broken by us
   the whole of humanity is held together by contracts
   and is suffocated by those contracts
stands up and goes to the portrait of his father, turning to his
   astonished sisters he takes his father's portrait down from the
   wall, holding it in front of him he says
   This was the moment I feared
   when I should have to take exactly the same place
   that I sat in all through my childhood
   and most of my youth
   opposite my father
   I always hated him
   I wished him dead
   his death had no effect on my hatred
putting the portrait on the floor he says while looking at the other
   portraits hanging on the wall
   All odious people
   from whom we have everything
   There is no reason
   to resume contact with the dead again
   Those who spawned us
   have ill rewarded us
   for being their children
   We are after all not the product of their minds
sitting down at the table exactly opposite the place where he was
   sitting before he got up
   It's true isn't it
   it's nothing more than calculated mockery
Dene *rises and brings his china and cutlery to him from the place*
   where he had been sitting before
Voss *while his sister is once again pouring gravy on to his plate*
   The dining room

the source of every calamity
Father mother children
nothing but players in hell
everything of any value
was always drowned
in soups and sauces
whenever I had a real thought
whenever I had a valuable thought
mother drowned it in her soup
whenever I had a real feeling
whenever I had a valuable feeling
she smothered it in her sauce
And father unscrupulously tolerated
what mother killed in me
that's why I hated this dining room
always hated it
nothing but death sentences were pronounced
from this place
from father's place
your fate was no different
but I wasn't as crafty as you two
I always fell into the trap
with a more or less cool head
Our parents weren't ashamed
not even mother
although shame should have been her duty
I really had to hate them and hate them all my life
in order to save myself
first the English detour
then the Norwegian one
thought Cambridge University was the answer
then thought the log cabin in Sognefjord was
we give everything up
in order to gain everything
and at the end we are worth less than at the beginning
To think we made music together
as though it had been thousands of years ago
to his older sister
What about it
do you still play the viola now and then
Dene
No no
Voss
We give up almost everything

when we give up
the instrument
which we have learned to play
Acting
is really a coarse art after all
playing an instrument is an entirely different matter
when an actor speaks
I have the constant feeling
that the world is a vulgar place
it's quite different from the way I feel
when a viola player plays the viola
or even just the piano as far as I'm concerned
if it's played well of course
to his older sister
Only a few weeks ago
I had an idea
of going back to Norway
but now I'm too weak for that
And besides that of course I have no reason
to go back to Norway
Dene
Why don't we just wait and see
what Doctor Frege says
Voss
Frege
what makes you think of Doctor Frege
Dene
I've made an appointment for you
for tomorrow afternoon
Voss
Nonsense
there's no point
in my going to Doctor Frege
the man is a fool
he's worse even than all the others
he drove our parents
into an early grave too
there are doctors
who only accelerate disease
exclaiming
Frege what a bungler
to his sister
And you've made an appointment for me
for tomorrow afternoon

I'm not going
to his younger sister
    What do you say about that
    your sister simply announces
    that tomorrow afternoon
    I am to go to see Doctor Frege
    I'm not going to any more doctors
    I'm not consulting any more doctors
Dene
    Aren't you going to eat any more
Ritter
    Oh do leave him in peace
    it really isn't so wonderful
    that we can't resist it
Dene
    I'm sure it isn't
    since you two have
    hardly eaten anything
rises and begins to clear the table
Voss
    I remember
    the last time Frege was here in the house
    and I was present
    that archbishop was also here
    those people suit each other
    a man like Frege
    ruthless obtuse
    and a man like that archbishop
    devious through and through
    Those Freges etcetera
    are horrible people
    who we are constantly running away from
    but who catch up with us time and time again
    at first it's our parents
    then it's our teachers
    then it's those Freges etcetera
Dene *goes out*
Ritter *rises and follows her*
Voss *shouting after them*
    You'd better beware of that Frege
    of those doctors and those medical superintendents
    especially the specialists
    All those people obfuscate

the areas in which we have less and less
freedom of movement
looking round
Always hated
always detested
art nouveau perversity
rising and going to the window, looking out and holding his head in
his hands
English intensity
Norwegian concentration
turning round and looking at the door through which his sisters have
exited, shouting
I'm not going to see Doctor Frege
How dare you
make an appointment for me with Doctor Frege
agitated
To go behind my back with Doctor Frege
pressing his hands to his head
Inability to concentrate
sitting down again at the table, shouting
Can't I even get a glass of water
in this house
Dene *enters and brings him a glass of water*
Voss
Frege that murderous Frege
greedily downing the water
No doctor please
please no doctor
they've all spelled nothing but misfortune for me
I want to kick the bucket on my own
without doctors
Dene *clearing the table*
Your post-prandial
states of exhaustion
takes the glass from her brother
Voss
Not Frege
straightening up to his full height
Frege no
collapses
Dene
The director thought
that the first few days would be the hardest

You ought to lie down after meals
I've made a wonderful dessert
all by myself
not Anna
I did
cream puffs
your favorite dessert
Ritter *enters with a large plate with cream puffs and puts it on the
    table*
Cream puffs fresh from the oven
Ritter *sits down*
Dene
Everything will be running smoothly soon
it all takes time
putting the dessert plates on the table
Of course you're exhausted
Voss
But I'm not exhausted
what do you mean exhausted
straightening up to his full height
a state of excitement
collapsing
isn't exhaustion at all
straightening up
The name Frege
ought not to have been mentioned
collapses
Dene *sits down*
Voss
That Frege
Dene
I spoke to the director
I said
what sort of doctor is best for my brother
in his present condition
serving the cream puffs
Frege said the director
my colleague Frege of course
Voss
I don't want a doctor
straightening up
least of all Frege
tugging very gently at the tablecloth
Incompetent people

The director too is incompetent
they charge exorbitant sums of money
and are totally incompetent
pulling at the tablecloth
Embroidered
by grandmother
wasn't it
Dene
Of course
by grandmother
all our beautiful tablecloths
were embroidered by our grandmother
during summer vacations
Voss
During summer vacations
they were always embroidering
and reading biographies of musicians
weren't they
tugging harder at the tablecloth
No no
self-control is everything
never lose your self-control
we hate everything that's embroidered
even if grandmother embroidered it
Ritter *bursts into loud laughter*
Voss
There are some who embroider
there are some who philosophize their way
through life
but they are all only hiding behind
an absurdity
and of course a lack of taste
tugs at the tablecloth very gently
Dene
Cream puffs fresh from the oven
that you are so fond of
Voss
Cream puffs
that I am so fond of
Ludwig
who's fond of cream puffs
who's fonder of cream puffs than of anything else
The whole time I was in Steinhof
I thought of nothing but those cream puffs

looking round
  It's like the inside of a tomb here
  we're really already buried
  a delicious tomb
  in which cream puffs are served
sniffing at his cream puffs
  the typical cream puff aroma
to his younger sister
  that's right
  isn't it
  they are freshly made for us
  so that we'll finish them up
exclaiming
  The highest art is the art of baking
Ritter *bursts into loud laughter*
Voss *sniffing at his cream puffs once again*
  When we eat them for the first time yes
  but then
  then they grow more and more insipid
  and finally we end up hating them
  and then we hate nothing more
  than cream puffs
  even if we are continually told
  that we are fonder of cream puffs
  than of anything else
to his older sister
  You expect me to eat these cream puffs
  yes perhaps I'll even eat a cream puff
  perhaps
  the devil says
  eat the cream puff
  which your sister has baked
  the devil says so
  the devil says so
  and Ludwig eats it
Ritter *bursts into laughter*
Voss
  Ludwig is eating the cream puff
  that his sister has baked
  the older sister baked it
  the younger sister served it
  and now they are both waiting
  to see me eat their cream puff
over-emphatically

What-is-put-before-us
If we take into account that
with all those cream puffs
with all those soups and sauces
we have become old and ugly and dull witted and worthless
then it's completely logical
for us to eat these cream puffs too
every cream puff
that is ever put on the table in front of us
*grabbing a cream puff from his plate and eating it like an animal in
one gulp and choking on it*
We wolf it down this cream puff
that our sister has baked
we open our mouth wide
and stick the cream puff in
and choke it down
to his older sister, while choking down the cream puff
You see how I'm choking down
your cream puff
such a nauseating cream puff
such a revolting cream puff
my favorite dessert
you see
Dene *jumps up and is about to run out but stops at the door shocked
to see that her brother is putting yet another cream puff into
his mouth*
Voss
And now for the second cream puff
the favorite dessert
my favorite dessert
that my sister has always made for me
Ritter *takes a bite of her cream puff*
Voss
My favorite dessert
my favorite dessert
*he chokes until he has swallowed half of the cream puff and then
suddenly spits out the second half pounding the table with the
flat of his hands in a rage*
Dene *turns and runs out*
Voss *to Ritter*
My favorite dessert
bangs his head on the table
Ritter *has jumped up and gone to him*
Voss *motionless*

Go away
go away you
don't touch me
Ritter *retreats, looks into the kitchen, goes back to her chair, sits down and finishes her cream puff*
Voss *straightens up to his full height and jerks the tablecloth toward him so that everything on the table is scattered on the floor*
Dene *rushes in*
Voss *into her face*
An étude my child
so that I don't lose my touch
only an étude
he lowers his head and rests it on the table
Dene and **Ritter** *stoop to pick up the china and cutlery from the floor*
Dene *runs out and returns with a whisk broom and a bucket, sweeps everything up and throws it into the bucket*
Voss *after a pause, motionless*
I keep wondering
how late it is
pressing his head with both hands and babbling
To lend meaning to life
Dene *and* **Ritter** *exit*
Voss *babbling*
To lend meaning to life
Dene *rushes in to fetch the tablecloth, presses it to her, turns and runs out with it*
Voss *raising his head and looking after her*
They get so upset those two
hissing
parasites
screaming
histrionic perversity
he seizes the large lamp and hurls it against the double door leading to the kitchen.

CURTAIN

After Dinner

The same as before dinner
Voss *sits at the table, facing the portrait of his mother*

Ritter *smoking a cigarette, drinking white wine, is seated in an*
armchair by the wall
You heard right
fifty-one percent
with that
fifty-one percent
our father bought our way into dramatic art
looking to the future so to speak
Father really had a genius for business
and he knew what was essential for us
It was just you he didn't know what to do with
all his life he didn't
taking a sip
With this fifty-one percent
we still decide to this day
when to perform
and when not
whether in a Shakespeare
or not
Voss
Bought our way into dramatic art
that's a clever remark
Ritter
That fifty-one percent
makes it possible for us
to employ our talent only
when we see fit
We do not allow ourselves to be cast arbitrarily
and shamelessly
we do not allow ourselves to be exploited unscrupulously
and wasted
The theatre manager is dependent on us so to speak
not we on him
taking a sip
And if for years at a time we don't feel like acting
we don't act
and if we do feel like it
we act Shakespeare etcetera
or a blind woman in an insipid play
on the stage for two minutes
The art of the theatre is independent only
when it owns fifty-one percent of the shares
to be honest
I only feel the urge to act

every few years
but that's not to say
that I neglect my talent
even for a single day
for two months our sister has been rehearsing the blind woman
in front of the window
and since she has to dance for one minute
out of the two
she's taking dance lessons
where she's learning
how a blind woman dances
that's not nearly as easy as you think
we are probably the only ones
who prepare themselves for their appearance down to the last detail
taking a sip
We have the time
to intensify ourselves
Voss *who keeps returning his gaze to the portrait of the mother*
The three of us
have never been compatible
too high-strung
too extraordinary
Siblings united in intelligence
in fact detested by everyone
or at least always objects of suspicion
Weirdness
that's what they've always accused us of
my spiritual Titanism indubitably
the highest aspiration
longing for humanity suicidal
all three
When we think
we can rest easy
we grow restless
Wealth bestowed by chance
which has made all the others incompetent
we allow ourselves be talked into things
delude ourselves
that we can be saved
longing for humanity suicidal
taking a notebook out of his coat pocket, opening it and reading
Did everything wrong up till today
Twelfth of July

that was two days ago
putting his notebook away again
So many errors accumulated
standing up and going to the portrait of his mother pointing to a part of
*   her face*
Here
you have that too
That's what we think about
all our lives
about nothing else
until we give up
because it makes no sense
can make no sense
whispering
Between you and me
I'm not going to Frege
I hate Frege
I hate doctors
but I hate that Doctor Frege
most of all
Those people are constantly burying us
in their garbage
see nothing think nothing
behave like murderers
and call themselves family doctors
looking at the mother's portrait
Mother
was the malicious one
not father
mother is the culprit
not father
sitting down
Went a little way with Schopenhauer
with Nietzsche
pernicious friendships
paper ties
book brothers
printed love affairs
In the end nothing
but nauseating
We enter books
as we enter taverns
hungry thirsty

starving my child
At first we are received with kindness
are waited on
but waited on worse and worse
waited on worse and still worse
and finally kicked out
or else we leave the taverns at once of our own accord
because we can't put up with the stench in them any longer
the badly cooked food
the miserably served food
but not of course
without paying a monstrous bill

Ritter *takes a sip pours out another glass of wine for herself*
Voss

We enter those philosophies
as we do open taverns
and sit down at once at the regulars' table
and we are surprised
that we are not waited on at once
to our most complete satisfaction
We are thoroughly annoyed
not least by the odious people
who are throwing their weight around with us in this tavern
We call for the landlord
but the landlord doesn't come
and even if at first
we were possibly enthusiastic
delighted possibly with the decor of the tavern
we start to loathe it after a very short time
we are badly seated
there's a draft
a noisome smell hangs in the air
instead of the most delicate aroma of roasting meat which we had
expected
We are served by small odious waiters
who have learned nothing
and who spend their time running around in their dull-witted way
and then finally bring everything to the table
except the things
that we have ordered
The food is inedible
the drinks poisoned
and then

when we try to call the landlord to account
we are told
that the landlord has been dead these many years
That's how we enter the great names
which promised us a philosophical repast
and it always turns out to be inedible
We enter books as we do taverns
that's our misfortune
Ritter *takes a sip*
Voss
We end up avoiding all taverns
don't go into them any more
no matter how dazzling the sign outside
we walk past it
after a pause
It turns out
that there are no tavern-owners left
only unscrupulous tenants
after a pause during which he looks at the mother's portrait
Mother
loved you two more
than me
Father hated me
but I loved him
that's the truth
The youngest girl is always loved
the most
pampered
that's her death sentence
exclaiming
Autarky
that's what father always
ended up
saying
Have enough coal in the cellar
for the next three winters
I can still hear him saying it
and also
philosopher philosopher
he isn't even good enough to be
an actor
Crafty sisters
who were in the end much cleverer

than he
Head of an industrial tycoon
that's what his brother said of him
Ritter *inquiringly*
Uncle Friedrich
Voss
No Uncle Karl
The humorous fellow
as opposed to
the humorless one
looking alternately at two portraits on the wall
Painters are dull-witted too
even when they are highly paid
even when they are highly renowned
Uncle Friedrich
is depicted as the humorous one
Karl as the humorless
exactly the opposite is true
Painters simply have no eye
looking at the portraits on the walls one after the other
They all had their portraits painted
the fools
standing up and taking the portrait of his mother down from the wall
   pressing it tightly to himself with both hands
This is where it belongs
not there
hanging it up where his father's portrait was previously and hanging
   his father's portrait up in exactly the same place that he has just
   taken his mother's from
It really is a perversity
that for thirty years these pictures
have been hanging on these walls
exactly opposite each other
in this perverse manner
not once taken down
But now it's equally perverse
don't you agree
that they are hanging opposite each other
badly painted
very badly painted
famous artists
but badly painted
wretchedly painted
taking his mother's portrait down and leaning it up against the wall

and also taking the father's portrait down and leaning it up
    against the wall
Portrait fixation
ancestor worship
taking the portrait of Uncle Karl off the wall and then the portrait of
    Uncle Friedrich and hanging it up in the place that he has taken
    Uncle Karl's portrait from, then taking Karl's portrait and then
    Friedrich's again, finally sitting down at the table exhausted
They have always made us suffer
these hideous pictures
The pictures are worth a fortune
millions
but they are hideous
sometimes they are more in fashion
sometimes less
but they are always worth millions
how hideous these pictures are
Wasn't mother
a beautiful woman
attractive
but in the picture she is repellent
she was malicious
but in the picture she looks lovable
father didn't brood
as he appears to in the picture
Those artists abuse everything
without the least shame
they will paint
one intolerable painting after another
to get their millions
A musical family
so it has always been said
it's not even hinted at
in any of these pictures
Have their portraits painted
that was the idea that kept haunting them
rising and asking his sister directly
You haven't had your portraits painted too
you didn't get taken in I hope
by a portrait-painting charlatan like that
Have you had your portraits painted or not
furiously
You did have your portraits painted
you're shameless enough

to have had your portraits painted
by those anti-artists
who are springing up everywhere today
and who chum up to people
and demand millions for their repellent daubs
You did have your portraits painted
Ritter
And what if we did
Voss
That was all I needed
my sisters
having their portraits painted
in this period of anti-art
in this epoch of dilettantism
where are those trumperies then
where are the trumperies
Ritter
In the attic
are you satisfied now
Voss
In the attic
in the attic
do portraits belong in the attic
Portraits don't belong in the attic
you hid them in the attic
so that I shouldn't see them
to conceal them from me
all the time I've been away
they've probably been hanging somewhere
on this wall
you took them down
and put them up in the attic
before I came here
just yesterday
just this morning
that's the truth
sits down exhausted
Ritter
The pictures are badly painted
Voss
Of course the pictures are badly painted
portraits are always badly painted
unless they're by Goya

but Goya didn't paint you
Goya never painted in Vienna
never did Goya paint in Vienna
suddenly sitting up straight
   I want to see them
   bring me the pictures
   bring the pictures this instant
Ritter *has jumped up*
Voss
   Bring the pictures
   bring me the pictures
   this instant
Ritter *takes a sip*
   What are you waiting for
   I said bring the pictures
   bring me the pictures
   which cost a fortune probably
Ritter *exits*
Voss *to himself*
   Having their portraits painted
   having their portraits painted for a fortune
   having their portraits painted for so much money
exclaiming through the door
   Millions of children are starving in Africa
   and you have your portraits painted
to himself
   Having their portraits painted
   my sisters having their portraits painted
   just as their parents had their portraits painted
   Odious patronage
exclaiming through the door
   Bring me the pictures
   I want to see the pictures
to himself, looking around
   Empty walls I've always liked
   empty walls
   This gallery full of atrocities
   has always turned my stomach
*rising to hang the portrait of his father in the place from which he had
     taken Uncle Friedrich's portrait, he hangs Uncle Karl's portrait
     where he took his father's portrait from*
to himself
   Hideous pictures

unartistic
insipid
Having their portraits painted
they've had their portraits painted
Art of painting
a base form of art
base to the core
sitting down
Consorting with painters
exclaiming
With painters
they grow rich and wealthy
and consort with those painters
And then that riffraff sits about everywhere
fouling the air
painters' effluvium
artistic whitewash
rising to take a girl's portrait down from the wall
This one perhaps
scrutinizing the picture
possibly
scrutinizing it intently
may be
no
it's not art
not art no
laying the picture down roughly on the table, sitting down
Music yes
painting no
looking at all the pictures one by one
It's all very arty
in keeping with the times
Dene *and* **Ritter** *enter with their portraits*
Voss
You've had your portraits painted
portraits painted
Dene *and* **Ritter** *show only the backs of the pictures*
Voss
But why don't you turn them round
do turn them round
if indeed we're dealing with works of art here
probably
by a famous artist

The contemporary
has always repelled me
Show yourselves
what do you look like
how did your artist paint you

Ritter *and* **Dene** *show him the fronts of their portraits*
Voss
And then my sisters expect me to forgive them
for this tastelessness
I don't feel like doing that
nauseating mannerism
I won't ask what these atrocities cost
just as though one of those people who go around in Rolls-Royces
had painted them

Ritter *and* **Dene** *put the portraits by the wall*
Voss
Having your portraits painted
and consorting with shamelessness itself
Ritter
I don't think the pictures are so bad
Voss
Not so bad
you don't think they're so bad
Ritter
You've never been able to relate
to painting
Voss
Not been able never been able
never able
Ritter
Never been able
Voss
And why did you hide
the pictures in the attic
surely not
because they are so magnificent
Hideous
and not even good likenesses
of you
and unartistic
Ritter
A young artist
a very young painter

Dene
    A friend of Doctor Frege
    put him in touch with Frege
Voss
    put him in touch with Frege
Ritter
    A young American
Dene
    Whose grandparents
    emigrated to America
    from Germany
Ritter
    A talented artist
Voss *rising and picking up the portraits of his sisters and looking at*
    But this is a declaration of bankruptcy
    a declaration of bankruptcy
throwing his sisters' portraits onto the table
    A fortune
    for a piece of vulgarity
looking at the pictures on the floor
    In comparison even those trumperies
    are works of art
sits down
Dene *takes the sisters' portraits*
Ritter *indicates to her that she should take them out*
Dene *takes them out*
Voss
    I cannot even say
    disfigured beyond recognition
    for that would at least be something
Ritter
    It was only to help
    a young artist that was all
Voss
    Young artists cannot be helped
    there is no greater folly
    than helping young artists
    helping artists at all
    is folly
    Let artists help themselves
    above all let young artists
    help themselves
    that's precisely why young artists come to nothing
    because they are constantly being helped

help an artist
and you destroy him
above all help a young artist
and you destroy and annihilate him
that's the truth
There is nothing more repellent
than assuming the cloak of patronage
But what is said
is not heard
I have always loathed
patronage
Wealthy people
patrons
hypocrites
resting his head in his hands
Visiting the brother in Steinhof
nothing but hypocrisy
going behind his back at home
having your portraits painted
having your portraits painted
and then even hanging up what was painted
and when your brother comes home
taking down what was hung up from the walls
and hiding it in the attic
suddenly
It was her idea
wasn't it
not yours
Ritter
It was my idea
Doctor Frege
Voss
Doctor Frege
suggested it to you
Ritter
Yes Doctor Frege
Voss
Doctor Frege Doctor Frege Doctor Frege
As if it weren't enough that he ruined your brother
he also makes arrangements for you
to have your portraits painted
But while those atrocities
were entered into the annals of art history long ago
looking at the pictures on the floor

these trumperies will not be entered into the annals of art history
this era will not be entered into the annals of art history
as a shameful blot of emptiness yes
as a catastrophe yes
as an artistic catastrophe
as a gigantic art crater
into which people will peer a hundred years from now
and from which there will issue nothing but a stench
nothing else
nothing else
nothing else
looking round
Empty walls that's what I always said
my Norwegian log cabin
is quite empty too
no pictures nothing
Empty walls
*rising and taking the remaining pictures from the walls and placing
them upright on the floor one after the other*
But of course
it will have to be repainted
or freshly wallpapered
for fifty years not one single fresh coat of paint
nothing wallpapered
this smell
*looking at the places on the wallpaper from which he has removed
the pictures*
That's what it looked like once
the wallpaper
Wasn't any better either
The new is still more hideous
And in any case it's time
something was changed here for once
Dene *enters*
Voss
The house belongs to us
not to the dead any more
trying to move the sideboard but he cannot
Why aren't you two helping
help me for heaven's sake
Ritter *and* **Dene** *try to push the sideboard with him but they fail*
Voss
Come on push for heaven's sake
push for heaven's sake

Ritter *and* **Dene** *try to push but it is no use*
Voss
    Half a meter to the left
    half a meter
    only half a meter
They all push but the sideboard does not budge
Voss
    Only half a meter
    perhaps it's nailed down
bending down and looking under the sideboard
getting up again
    Push
    only half a meter
the sideboard does not budge
    Push
    Concentrate and push
They all push jerkily and inside the sideboard china can be heard
    falling over
Ritter *bursts out into loud laughter*
Dene
    Dreadful
Voss
    No wonder
    gently push very gently
    that's what I said
    not jerkily
    steadily but not jerkily
sits down at the table exhausted
Dene *opening the doors of the sideboard and gradually taking out a*
    heap of broken pieces of china
    The beautiful Herend plates
    the beautiful Bohemian teapot
    good lord
turning to her brother
    The most beautiful pieces all broken
Ritter *has seated herself on the armchair by the window and lit a cigarette*
Dene
    The most beautiful pieces
Voss
    Gently I said
    steadily but gently
    not jerkily
Dene *exits and returns with a dustpan and the whisk broom and*
    sweeps up the pieces

Voss *who has been looking at the clock for a long time*
  If only
  we could move the clock just half a meter to the left
  it would be something of an improvement
  but I'll do that on my own
Dene
  But why do you want to move the clock
Voss
  For as long as I can think
  it has bothered me
  that the clock stands there
  Just half a meter to the left
  just to try it perhaps
going to the clock and pushing it a little to the left
stepping back and looking at it
going back as far as possible and looking at it
  No
  no good
  no good
*going to the clock and pushing it back to its original place then taking
    a step back and looking at it*
  The clock
  probably doesn't belong
  in the dining room at all
  it's a dirty trick
  having a clock in the dining room
  What do you say
  where shall we put the clock
  but the clock must go
  I can't bear the sight of the clock
sits down at the table
Dene *exits with the broken pieces of china*
Ritter
  Perhaps in the small drawing room
  there is no clock in the small drawing room
Voss
  Right there isn't a clock in the small drawing room
  It will go well in there
  in the small drawing room
Ritter *rises and presses a knob on the record player and sits
    down again*
Beethoven string quartet very softly
Voss *staring at the clock*
  In the small drawing room

you're right
that's where it belongs
it's insipid in the dining room
and besides it doesn't even keep time
it's half an hour fast
and it has to be wound up every other day
Dene *enters and sits down in an armchair some distance from* **Ritter**
Voss *looking at the ceiling*
One day it will collapse
and kill you
But I won't be around to see it
looking along the walls
Whitewash is healthy
fresh whitewash
white fresh whitewash
Father already suffered from a hatred of wallpaper
Women are in favor of wallpaper
hate whitewash
women hate whitewash
that's been proven
Dene *gets up and picks up two or three pieces of broken china which*
she had missed before
Voss
There are those who hate wallpaper
and those who hate whitewash
without more ado we can divide humanity
into these two groups
into the group that hates wallpaper
and into the group
that hates whitewash
suddenly
The string quartets
have always calmed me
I am allowed to play them for myself
as often as I like
said the director
he was corruptible too
I put horrendous sums in his coat pocket
these people will take any amount of money
I'm allowed to listen to the string quartets
I'm allowed to read
I'm allowed to *occupy myself intellectually*
as the director always says
Rich people live on bribery

And about eight I listen to the *Eroica*
conducted by Knappertsbusch
taking his notebook out of his coat pocket and reading
Twenty-seventh of May *Eroica*
twenty-eighth of May *Eroica*
twenty-ninth of May *Eroica*
thirtieth of May *Eroica*
thirty-first of May *Eroica*
first of June *Eroica* etcetera
turning a few pages and reading
Older sister
Logic One
transcribed like a good girl
shutting his notebook
Exact bookkeeping
extraordinarily exact bookkeeping
opening his notebook, leafing through it, reading
Older sister
tastelessly dressed as always
sits there for hours
doesn't say a word
doesn't understand anything
younger sister
never seen her on the stage
probably no talent exclamation mark
like the older one exclamation mark
but they keep getting another chance
because father
bought fifty-one percent of the shares
in the theatre
in which they appear from time to time
parenthesis out of sheer boredom
pre-war shares
closing his notebook putting it away again
A sample
Dene *exits*
Ritter *lighting a cigarette*
Our brooder
our know-it-all
our charming note-taker
Voss
When I'm in London
I say to myself
Norway is the place

when I'm in Norway
I say to myself London
then when I don't know how to go on
to Steinhof
But I have not been declared legally incompetent
that should give you something to think about
I'm the only one in Steinhof
who has not been declared legally incompetent
I enjoy a fool's license little sister
Ritter
It's possible
Voss
Possible you say
possible
I always think that you are totally without talent
and then time and again
that you are the most talented of all
on the stage
She's so easily hurt
your sister
a trifle
and she's insulted
upset
anyway
we don't do people any harm
and they are angry with us
she's probably doing the dishes
ironing
Ritter
She took a lot of trouble
to make things nice for you
she wanted to make your return
more pleasant
Voss
More pleasant
make things nice
female stupidities
I said
I'm going home for just a few days
only a few days I said
what's it like here
that's what I wanted to see
but it's just
as I imagined

And also because I was looking for a book
a particular copy of Schopenhauer
but I can't find it
a lot of books missing
God knows what's become of the books
I want to talk to her
but she's in a hurry
Whispering with the director behind my back
about Frege
to deliver me up to that man
who calls himself a family doctor
We go to him
because our bladder hurts
and he looks into our ears
we tell him we have a pain in our right knee
he percusses our chest
and because we have no medical insurance
we spend a fortune on these people
enormous consumption of specialists
medicine is a perverse preservation of monuments
As it's now in fashion again
to cut your hair short
I'm letting mine grow
I don't follow fashion
fashion is something I've always hated
the two of you follow fashion
stretching out his legs taking his notebook from his pocket, leafing
through it, reading
A world which constantly
confuses cause and effect
Suffer from megalomania
that's right
trusted Schopenhauer
trusted Nietzsche
never trusted myself
time and time again I was suddenly
abandoned by everybody
Next I wrote
polished my shoes at half past two in the morning
shutting his notebook and putting it away again
Histrionics
Calumny
World of entertainment

Ritter *lights a cigarette*
Voss
    Your sister
    suffers from paranoia
    a fetish for dishes
    porcelain disease
    Make things nice
    by putting cream puffs
    on the table in front of me
    and at the same time doesn't want to listen
    to what I'm saying
    despises my inmost being
    but insists
    that I eat her cream puffs
    As you can see I do eat them
    with disgust
    Not going to Doctor Frege
    Frege's to blame
    for my being sick in the first place
inquiringly
    Am I sick
    I am sick
    I am not sick
    I tell your sister
    I want to go to a concert
    she takes out a season's subscription
    I tell her I want a cream puff
    and she regales me with dozens of them
    I say I want to be left in peace
    and she keeps on asking me
    whether I want to be left in peace
    If we made one mistake
    we made thousands of mistakes
    if we fell into the brook once
    we fell into the brook many many times
    if we told one lie once
    we've been liars all our lives
    Whatever we do and whatever we say
    is multiplied in the most diabolical fashion
    But she transcribes my manuscripts carefully
    I must grant her that
whispering
    But I'm very stingy with my praise
    if we praise someone

we are immediately exploited
if we say something complimentary about someone
we immediately pay the price
sitting up and looking at the ceiling
An earthquake to be sure
would have devastating consequences
but the old houses
don't collapse as we know
look at San Francisco
look at San Francisco
I wish this country
would disappear one day
or better still
some night all of a sudden
in an earthquake
this odious fatherland
off the face of the earth
Then again I think
we haven't got a better one
rising and going to his sister and showing her his hand
Here you see
where I burned myself
a burn wound
not unintentionally
I held the candle
under my hand until
it was half burnt through
and here on my neck
showing it
I still have the marks
of my strangulation attempt
What have we here
asked the resident
in his sly manner
A strangulation attempt
last night
I replied
at which he laughed out loud
Then why on earth didn't you hang yourself *properly*
said the resident
Do you think I'm crazy
I replied
I'm not going to hang myself
you must know that

a strangulation attempt doesn't mean
that I intend
to hang myself
no no I said
as you know
everything
which concerns me
bogs down in the attempt
at which the resident laughed out loud again
There's a thousand schilling bill for you
I said to him
and now be off
he took the thousand schilling bill
and went off
whispering
The residents are corruptible
and the residents' assistants
are the most easily corrupted
It's only because I feed them all thousand schilling bills
that I'm still alive
Steinhof is an institution of corruption
Those who haven't got any money
don't survive long
that's the truth
they hate every new arrival
they look forward to mine
Worringer's coming
runs like wildfire through Steinhof
it resounds through the whole institution
Worringer the millionaire is coming
that's what they say
then all those white coats rush in
and bow and scrape
and let me feed them
If I were to say
they should wipe my behind
as I want it done
of course as I want it done
they would fight for the privilege of doing it
In return I let them abuse me by calling me a philosopher
which they have long since grown accustomed to doing
Dene *enters with a pile of long cotton underpants*
Voss
And what have we got here

Dene
    I bought you some new underpants
Voss *examines the underpants*
Dene
    Freshly laundered and ironed
Voss
    But these are wonderful cotton underpants
    I wonder if they'll fit
Dene *taking one of the pairs of underpants and giving it to him*
    They're your size
Voss
    My size
Ritter *laughs out loud, rises and turns down the volume of the*
    string quartet
Voss
    My size you say
    my size
holding the pair of underpants out in front of him looking at the floor
    My size
    may be my size
Ritter *sits down again*
Voss
    But aren't they too soft
    I hate soft underpants
    I've always hated them
    all my life
    I had underpants which were too soft
Dene
    You always wore silk underpants
Voss
    Because my mother
    had got it into her head
    and I had got into the habit
    and never anything but silk underpants
Dene
    Very common coarse cotton underpants
Voss
    They are
Dene
    From Switzerland
Voss
    Swiss cotton underpants
    so-called Alpine cotton underpants

Ritter
  The dependable Mont Blanc underpants
Voss
  Mont Blanc underpants
  of course
  the dependable Mont Blanc underpants
  they really do fit
  if I had my way I put them on at once
inquiringly
  may I
Dene
  No no
  not here
  not now
  not here
  for heaven's sake not in the dining room
  here
  now
Ritter
  But why not
  If he wants to
  why on earth shouldn't he put on his underpants
  here and now
rising and touching the underpants which Voss is still holding,
      calling out
  Fabulous
  the dependable Mont Blanc underpants
  Go on put them on here
  why not for heaven's sake
Dene
  No you can't do that
Voss *takes off his coat and puts it on the table, unbuttons his fly and is*
      about to take his trousers off
Ritter
  That's simply preposterous
  why shouldn't he put on
  his underpants now
Dene
  Not while I'm here
  you can't do that
  give them to me
snatching the pair of underpants from his hands
  be sensible

Ritter
  Why did you bring the underpants in just now
  if he's not permitted to put them on
Voss
  Not permitted to
  not permitted to
  permission denied
Ritter *to him*
  You're not permitted to
  you heard didn't you
  you're not permitted to
Dene *to her sister*
  You have no shame
turns and exits
Ritter *calling after her*
  Silly idiot
to her brother
  She loves you
  unhappily
  now as always
  she hasn't changed
  she found out
  that you liked long coarse cotton underpants
  immediately she bought
  a pile of these long coarse underpants
Voss *does up his fly buttons again*
Ritter
  Why didn't you put on
  the underpants
  you should have taken off your trousers
  and put on your underpants
  Oh you disgust me both of you
returning to her seat, sitting down and lighting a cigarette
  You should have put on the underpants
  this false hypocritical modesty
Voss *puts on his coat*
Ritter
  Hypocritical from the day she was born
referring to her sister
  What do you think she's doing now
turning off the string quartet
  She's burying her face
  in the underpants
  which you held in your hands

Brings your underpants into the dining room
and then stops you
from putting your underpants on
suddenly agitated
Where did you burn yourself
Where
show me
I want to have another look
show me
Voss *goes to her*
Ritter *taking his hand and looking at the scar*
A big hole
looking into his face
With the candle you say
burned your own hand
your own
Probably in the middle of the night
Voss *nods*
Ritter
Did it hurt very much
Voss *nods*
Ritter
But you didn't manage
to burn it right through
that would have been a triumph
to have burned right through your own hand
Voss *nods*
Ritter
In complete secrecy
*draws him to her and tries to kiss him; first he refuses, then he presses
her tightly to him to kiss her till they hear their sister approaching*
Ritter *pushing him away*
Have you lost your mind
you'll break my neck if you're not careful
Dene *has entered, asks*
Shall we drink
black coffee
Ritter
Yes of course
right Ludwig
Dene *exits again*
Voss *sits down at the table*
Ritter
Did you take a close look at her

going to the record player and putting on the Eroica *conducted*
   by Knappertsbusch
   Just as I told you
Eroica *very softly*
   She buried her face
   in your underpants
   That's part of
   the therapy
   isn't it
   As long as father was alive
   we weren't allowed to play the *Eroica*
   Besides he hated Knappertsbusch
   he loved Furtwängler
sitting down again and stretching out her legs
   The Viennese all have
   a Beethoven complex
   a Schubert complex
   or a Beethoven complex
   that's what they're all infected with
   in the wealthy suburbs they're all infected with it
exclaiming
   We are all wealthy suburbanites
   wealthy suburbanites that's what we are
   Ludwig
   we are wealthy suburbanites
clatter of china as if the older sister had fallen down behind the
   kitchen door
Ritter *jumping up*
   Now she's even gone and fallen over
   the silly idiot
Voss *making to leave*
Ritter *pushing him back*
   stay here
opening the door
   Have you hurt yourself
   Good lord you're bleeding
   come here
Voss *watches the younger sister help the older one up*
Dene *after she has stood up*
   Lost my footing
Ritter
   Indeed
Dene
   Everything's driving me crazy

Ritter
    You're just too hard on yourself
Voss *turns around and goes to the table, turns around again and*
    watches the two sisters
Dene
    Pity about the coffee
Ritter
    Oh never mind
    it's a pity about the china
    about the china
Dene
    Grandmother's lovely china
Ritter
    It had to be grandmother's Bohemian china
Voss
    Nervousness is an affliction
Dene *and* **Ritter** *look at their brother*
Voss
    Probably a change in the weather
    trouble brewing
    probably
Ritter *and* **Dene** *scoop up the pieces of china*
Voss
    The things we like
    are all of a sudden strewn on the floor
    grandmother's lovely china
    A fatality mechanism
looking round while the two sisters are scooping up all the pieces
    of china
    I'm not going to Frege
    not to Frege
taking his notebook out of his coat pocket opening it and leafing
    through it and reading
    Sisters underlined in red
    infantilism
    excessive infantilism
snapping the notebook to and putting it back into his coat pocket
    The century of uncertainty
after a pause
    Total stultification at the turn of the millennium
Ritter *and* **Dene** *have stood up with the pieces of broken china*
Voss
    Congregation of hypocrites
    Chronic despondency

The director said
that a time would come
when even in Steinhof
there would be no more pea soup
Ritter *and* **Dene** *go out*
Voss *shouting after them*
Richesse oblige don't forget that
sitting down at the table and staring at the sideboard
Half a meter to the left
First clear it out
then push it
looking at the clock
The clock must go
fought for a hundred years against illiteracy
and achieved nothing
looking at the dining room ceiling
If we publish it
then we'll be dead
looking round
Always preferred cotton
rising he goes to the record player and turns up the Eroica *as loud as*
possible and hangs up the portraits which he has taken down
from the wall one after another all in places opposite their
original ones then, turning the Eroica *off altogether, he sinks*
totally exhausted into an armchair by the wall
They didn't give me my doctorate
in Cambridge
they were all against me
although I wanted the doctorate
I always said that I didn't want it
and yet I wanted it
I said I didn't want it
it was a farce
and yet I wanted it
with exaggerated precision
Wasn't given
to me
We're going astray with Schopenhauer
Ritter *and* **Dene** *enter with coffee and set the table*
Voss
Great need for geometry
great need for coffee
no need for company

Dene
>   I asked for size five
>   they didn't have it
>   I had to wait three days
>   everybody wants
>   this cotton underwear nowadays

Ritter
>   As we've got such a lot of china
>   it doesn't matter

Dene
>   True

Voss
>   A lot of sugar please

Ritter
>   Where is the sugar

Dene
>   I'll get it straightaway

exits

Ritter *lighting a cigarette*
>   Do you still own the Norwegian log cabin

Voss *nods*

Ritter
>   I thought
>   you'd sold it

Voss *shakes his head*

Ritter
>   And when are you going back to Norway

Voss
>   I don't know

Ritter
>   Let's see you had to climb up a cliff
>   even to get to it
>   you certainly can't do that any more
>   you're much too weak to do that you know

sitting down at the table
>   You are the only privileged person in Steinhof
>   You can do anything you want there
>   *almost* anything
>   That's because you pay seven thousand a day
>   they'll let you stay on in Steinhof for years and years

Dene *enters with a sugar bowl and puts it on the table*

Ritter *to her*
>   For heaven's sake do sit down

you're a bundle of nerves
it's not Ludwig who is
it's *you*
Ritter *and* **Dene** *discover that the pictures are now hanging on the*
   walls opposite their original places
Ritter *looking out of the window*
   Rainy afternoon in all likelihood
   best thing is to spend it in bed
Dene
   I'll do some ironing
Ritter
   There's nothing nicer
   than a rainy afternoon in bed
All three drink coffee

CURTAIN

Note: *Ritter, Dene, Voss intelligent actors.* During my work on the
play, which I completed two years after writing that note, my thoughts
dwelt mainly on my friend Paul and on his uncle, Ludwig
Wittgenstein. Th. B. June 1984

A WORD ABOUT *HISTRIONICS*

The German title of the play is *Der Theatermacher:* we have rendered this as *Histrionics* in order to try to preserve the double meaning of the original. In German *Theater machen* not only means to act or produce plays, but also "to make a scene." This is important for the director and the actor playing Bruscon to bear in mind. The play is, of course, open to any number of interpretations and can readily be seen on a number of levels as a searing criticism of bullying, hectoring dictatorship, whether in private or in public life, and Bernhard is certainly quite explicit in his references to Hitler. We may also want to bear in mind what Bernhard himself has said about actors in an interview in *Theater Heute* in October 1985.

"I despise actors," he says, "indeed I hate them, for they ally themselves at the least sign of danger with the audience and betray the author and completely identify with stupidity and feeble-mindedness. *Actors are the destroyers and exterminators of imagination,* not those who bring it to life and they are the true gravediggers of literature. Minetti (the creator of the role of Boris in *A Party for Boris*) is the exception."

Like Stoppard in the English theatre, Bernhard draws much of his imagery and metaphorics from the theatre. The irony of course is that Bruscon is both dramatist and actor in *Histrionics,* and Bernhard does indeed seem to be casting doubt both upon the grandiloquence of the actor and upon the theatre in general.

HISTRIONICS

A certain talent for the theatre
even as a child
a born man of the theatre you know
histrionic
setter of traps even very early in life

The Black Hart in Utzbach

Dance Hall

Dramatis Personae
Bruscon *A histrionic*
Madame Bruscon, *also a histrionic*
Ferruccio, *their son*
Sarah, *their daughter*
The Landlord
The Landlord's Wife
Erna, *their daughter*

Scene One

Three o'clock in the afternoon
Enter **Bruscon** *(the histrionic) and the* **Landlord**
Bruscon *wearing a broad-brimmed hat, an ankle-length coat, and
 carrying a cane*
 What here
 in this fusty atmosphere
 I might have known that it would come to this
exclaiming
 Nationally recognized actor[1]
 My God
 I used not to set foot in this sort of inn
 not even to pass water
 And they expect me to play my
 Wheel of History here
Taking a few steps to the right
 The Black Hart
 ah well
 it's as if time had stood still
Taking a few steps to the left, then speaking directly to the Landlord
 As if you hadn't known

---

1. The original refers to Bruscon as a *Staatsschauspieler.* This is a title given by the state
to outstanding actors. The closest analogy in the English-speaking world would probably
be the titles bestowed upon Gielgud, Edith Evans, Olivier, Richardson, etc., for "services
to the theatre."

that we were coming today
Looking round
Desolate
Looking round
Total lack of culture
desolate
He wants to sit down but there is no chair on the platform
Speaking directly to the Landlord
Utzbach
Utzbach like Butzbach
Bruscon, the nationally recognized actor
in Utzbach
My comedy in this wretched Utzbach
Looking round
Black Hart
ah well
It's so sultry
sultry there'll be a thunderstorm
Such a sensitive spirit
in such a sensitive body
Suddenly in a fury
Haven't you got a chair an armchair
The Landlord *brings an armchair*
Bruscon *sits*
Landlord
You said frittata soup
Bruscon
Naturally
That's the only thing
worth eating around here
frittata soup
But not too greasy
there's always all that fat floating on the soup
even in frittata soup
provincialism celebrates its triumphs
Stretching out his legs
In Gaspoltshofen
we had a huge success
dazzling
ideal conditions
looking round
Did my daughter Sarah tell you
that I must have
a second pillow

And it must be horsehair
But I'm sure you'll have no trouble
providing me with such a horsehair pillow
Landlord
The horsehair pillow
is already on the bed
Bruscon
Is already on the bed
you say
is already on the bed
Looking around
Theories do not accord
with practice
How many inhabitants did you say
Landlord
Two hundred and eighty
Bruscon
Two hundred and eighty
A midget community
Incredible
In Gaspoltshofen
we had eight hundred and thirty in the house
all paying full price
all of them applauding absolutely enthusiastically
If I had known
that this
this
Landlord
Utzbach
Bruscon
that this Utzbach
had only two hundred and eighty inhabitants
Old people
who can neither hear
nor see
Speaking directly to the Landlord
The Wheel of History
is a *humana comedia*
Spreading both arms out as wide as possible
Caesar Napoleon Churchill
appear
which is not to say
that the distaff side
is shortchanged

Basically I have
survived on nothing but frittata soup
on this whole tour
In Gaspoltshofen
it was absolutely extraordinarily tasty
Scarcely any fat
looking round
And of course Metternich
plays a decisive role
in my comedy
which in fact
is a tragedy
as you will see
The Landlord *begins pushing tables against the walls*
The nature of things
is always the opposite, my dear sir
We go off on a tour
but all we actually do is walk into a trap
so to speak into a theatre trap
Suddenly barking at the Landlord
Have you seen
the fire chief yet
about the emergency exit light
As I said
it must be pitch dark
at the end
of my comedy
even the emergency exit light must be out
pitch dark
perfectly dark
at the end of my comedy
if it's not perfectly dark
then my *Wheel of History* will be ruined
If the emergency exit light is not extinguished
then my comedy will be perverted
into its exact opposite
In Gaspoltshofen
they extinguished the emergency exit light
in Frankenmarkt as well
even in Ried im Innkreis
which after all is infamous for being one of the most stupid places
Tell the fire chief
that I am Bruscon
Bruscon the nationally recognized actor

who played Faust in Berlin
and Mephisto in Zurich
Firemen are pigheaded
statistics show
that every year they cause more havoc
than anyone else
Once a building's on fire
the firemen totally destroy it
This sultriness
Unbuttoning his coat to the waist
On the other hand I'll catch cold
if I take my coat off
Racked with coughing every moment of my life
tortured with sore throats
bathed in perspiration
The Landlord *starts to open a window*
Bruscon *brandishing his cane imperiously*
Don't you dare
do you want me to sit in a draft
huddling up
What a foul stench
Is there still money in pig breeding
The Landlord *closes the window again*
Bruscon
Or is it just innkeepers' perversity
This ubiquitous stench of pigs
From one pig breeding institute to another
The fact is there's nothing here
but pig breeding institutes
and churches
Groaning
and Nazis
Leaning back and closing his eyes
If we are not allowed
to switch off the emergency exit light
we shall not perform
Sitting up
This place is a scourge of God
And it's for this that I attended the academy
for this I was decorated
with the gold cross on the blue ribbon
Clutching his head
Agatha warned me
Getting up and looking around

Sooner or later the disaster was bound to happen
If we think clearly
we're bound to do away with ourselves
*Standing in the middle of the platform and holding his cane up as high
  as possible, staring at the ceiling of the hall*
Utzbach
*Lowering his arm and walking five paces to the right, then ten paces to
  the left, measuring the stage, stops*
The stage in Gaspoltshofen
was no larger
In Ried im Innkreis
it was two meters wider
but that was only a drawback
Directly to the Landlord
Actually for me
it's not such a disaster
as it is for my wife
she is allergic to the stench of pigs
because there's something wrong with her lungs
even in the purest air she has
difficulties
After all she has to make
a half-hour speech to the people of Rome
and no allowances made
clearing his throat
Every word here stirs up dust
and my comedy's
infernal text
calling into the hall
Your Excellency I regret
directly to the Landlord
More or less
a comedy of creation
without going so far as to call it
an epoch-making work
calling into the hall
Calabria
don't make me laugh
directly to the Landlord
A late work indubitably
Have you read about it
All nonsense
like everything in the newspapers

Incompetent hacks
bending down and testing the floor of the stage with his right hand
But not one of them tore it to bits
not one of them qualified
but not one of them tore it to bits
straightening up again
My wife
suffers from continual headaches
there's something wrong with my kidneys
bending over again and once again testing the floor of the stage
Just as long as we don't fall through
In Gaspoltshofen
they had a new floor
this one is all moldy and rotten
Don't you have dances here any more
straightening up again with difficulty
Don't you have dances on this platform any more
It doesn't look as if
anyone has danced on this platform
in recent years
It seems that only old people live here nowadays
and they don't dance
no theatrical performances here
for ages
to the Landlord
Would you please bring one of the tables up here
onto the platform
Our sets are virtually
nonexistent
as simple as can be
We use a screen three times
that's all
and a portal
The Landlord *brings a table on to the platform*
Bruscon
As you have noticed
we travel with only a trunk
and a laundry basket
nothing else
Over there
Put the table over there
The lighting
is what really counts

Landlord *places the table next to Bruscon*
Bruscon *motions to him with his cane to place the table in front of him*
Landlord *does as Bruscon indicates*
Bruscon
Our imagination even our intellect
have to be rearranged constantly
in the end nothing corresponds
Put the table there
pointing to where the table should be
Landlord *puts it there*
Bruscon
Yes
that's the place for the table
at least for the moment
for the moment
leaning back
Imagination
magic
sitting up straight again, while the **Landlord** *again starts pushing the*
tables in the hall back against the wall talking directly to the
Landlord
Do you know St. Radegund
Where is it
Landlord
It's ten kilometers further on
Bruscon
Ten kilometers
really
that's what I thought
Ten kilometers you say
Landlord
Ten kilometers
Bruscon
I was assaulted and knocked down there
in nineteen hundred and forty-four
by a butcher's assistant
who mistook me for a candlemaker
alleged to have hailed from Mattighofen
As a result I still have these pains in my shoulder
plaguing my life which would be burdensome enough
even without that episode
It's been forty years since that crime took place
I was still a student at the time

I was studying theatre history
not as you think
at a university
I was completely self-taught after all
I came into this area
I forget how
and was assaulted in St. Radegund
it might well have been the end of me
looking down at the floor
I wore extra long trousers
in those days
and a linen cap on my head
I called it my cap of advantage
for I soon found out
that it was an advantage to think
while wearing that cap
If I wanted to think clearly
I would put that cap on
that linen cap
which I had inherited from my grandfather
on my mother's side
And just imagine
I simply couldn't manage to think even in the city
without that linen cap of my grandfather's
at any rate not with the necessary clarity
which I have raised to a matter of principle
in the end I wore that cap all the time
that I was working on my comedy
If I take the cap off
my comedy will be ruined
that's what I always thought
and I kept it on
for the whole nine years
that I was working on my comedy
our *Wheel of History* that is
I tell you
unless the emergency exit light is switched off
we shan't perform
What sort of people are they anyway
these fire chiefs
It's simply ludicrous
that here in
in
in

Landlord
   In Utzbach
Bruscon
   In Utzbach
   there even is a fire chief
   in this hole of all holes
   you'll forgive me
   calling your village a hole
   I'm sure you hold it in high regard
   that there's a fire chief
   who refuses to allow
   the emergency exit light
   to be switched off
   for five minutes
   Really
   only five minutes without an emergency exit light
   at the end of my comedy
   Even in Ried im Innkreis
   there was no debate on that point
   The light grows dim
   finally very dim
   and finally it goes out completely
   naturally the emergency exit light as well
   The climax of my comedy
   is perfect darkness
   that is the sine qua non for the whole thing
   if it isn't to be perverted into its opposite
pulling his armchair right up to the table
   Churchill wakes up in the night
   before his death
   and his parting word is Elba
   and then it becomes perfectly dark
   My son Ferruccio by the way
   is a phenomenal Churchill
   Ferruccio you know
   because I am an admirer of Busoni
standing up and stamping on the floor
   In the scene with Stalin
   Churchill stamps on the floor
   it would be disastrous
   if the floor didn't hold
   The audience would inevitably
   burst out laughing

but that would be the end of my comedy
stamping on the floor again
  In Gaspoltshofen my son
  stamped on the floor with such emphasis
  that he injured his leg
  right up to the knee
  but the performance was not interrupted
  It caused a short break
  I as Stalin
  simply said some lines
  that we had originally cut
  then I picked up my son
  that is I picked up Churchill
  and carried him out
  I dragged him out more than carried him
  which gave rise to thunderous applause
going to the left wall and turning round
  Shakespeare
  Voltaire
  and I
taking three paces to the middle of the platform and looking into the
    hall
  I'm in the process
  of translating my comedy
  into Italian
  not the easiest of tasks my dear sir
  And while I'm about it
  possibly into French as well
  a language which I confess I'm infatuated with
  The Wheel of History is just as suited to
  Italy as to France
  it was written primarily for the French
  Here we are just trying it out
  we are developing it
  honing our skills
  I'm afraid my *Wheel of History*
  will be more successful in Italy
  than in France
going to the right wall and laying the flat of his hands on it
  I already had the idea for my play
  in Le Havre
  where I met my wife
  a coastal acquaintanceship so to speak

Atlantic coastal acquaintanceship
thrusting his cane up and calling into the hall
Bertrand
you are tempting fate
lowering his cane
The dampness here
muffles everything
Everything here
militates against the instrument
of the human voice
going to one of the windows and wiping the dust off the window sill
with his sleeve
Incidentally I was only fourteen
when I sketched out my comedy
The theme pursued me all my life to so speak
wiping the dust off the window sill once more
a sort of *theatrum mundi*
Thought which sought no reward you understand
stepping onto the platform and standing in the middle of it looking at
the hall
a certain talent for the theatre
even as a child
a born man of the theatre you know
histrionic
setter of traps even very early in life
bending down and testing the floor of the platform
getting up again
Broke away from home
cuffs on the ears blows
beaten over the head by my father
Total mutual contempt
bending over again and testing the platform
Sadistic in a certain sense
autosadistic
Worked my way up from the very bottom
getting up again and shouting into the hall
The poison is in Lörrach
The poison is stored in Lörrach
the poison which will wipe out humanity
directly to the Landlord
That my dear sir is the Lörrach effect
in my *Wheel of History*
sitting in the armchair
So-called power wielders

fire chiefs
In Gaspoltshofen
I had no trouble at all
directly to the Landlord
Tell the fire chief
that it's only a matter of five minutes
five decisive minutes to be sure
Tell him that
if at the end of my play
there are not five minutes of total darkness
my play will be ruined
that would make this place
the one exception
wiping the sweat from his forehead with a handkerchief
I am not inclined
to enter into a debate
with the fire chief
it's just a question of his agreeing
to five minutes of total darkness
five minutes with no emergency exit light
preposterous
leaning back
The whole world
into its nethermost recesses
is made bilious by absurd laws
This abominable hole
you don't even have fires here as you yourself admitted
there never has been a fire
it's preposterous
to insist that the emergency exit light cannot even be out for five
minutes
In this dampness
and since everything is rotten
there's no possibility of a fire breaking out
tell the fire chief that
What's his name anyway
Landlord
Attwenger
Bruscon
Attwenger
Herr Fireman Attwenger
Herr Fire Chief Attwenger
What does this fire chief Attwenger
do for a living anyway

Landlord
He's a wright
Bruscon
Wright wright
What sort of a wright
Landlord
Wheelwright
Bruscon
wheelwright
Just imagine there are still wheelwrights
in this day and age
wheelwright and fire chief
Go
and tell him who I am
and tell him
that his family will of course
get complimentary tickets
Landlord
The wheelwright doesn't have a family any longer
Bruscon
No longer
Then tell him
that he'll get a copy of my play
with my autograph
with Bruscon's autograph
Bruscon who never gives such autographs
who has always refused
to give such autographs
after all one of my personal autographs like that
will be worth a fortune one day
when I am known not only as Bruscon
the great actor but also as the great dramatist
and tell him
that he may dine with us
with us at our own table
tell him that
But how did they come to die on him
the family
Landlord
Struck by lightning sir
They went on an outing to Haag
and stood under a birch tree
they were all killed
except the wheelwright

Bruscon
　　And yet they always say
　　if you're in the lurch find a birch
leaning back, his eyes shut
　　Tell you what landlord
　　before you go to the fire chief
　　order us some frittata soup
　　from the kitchen
　　four frittata soups
　　if that's possible
　　at this time
　　but of course your wife is in the kitchen
　　I noticed her
　　of course it's unusual
　　to order frittata soup
　　at half past three in the afternoon
　　We'll eat the frittata soup
　　here on the platform
　　on this table
　　my son my daughter and I
　　send my wife's frittata soup
　　up to her room
　　poor woman she's still in a state of shock
　　Utzbach
　　it's a charming place from the sound of it
　　she said on her way here
　　and then when she saw Utzbach
　　she fainted
　　Histrionic type of course
　　On the other hand it's just as well
　　if she retires before the performance
　　otherwise she'll forget her lines
　　she forgets her lines all the time
　　we've been playing the same thing for years
　　and she still always loses her lines
　　and always at crucial points
　　my dear sir, it could drive you mad
　　You simply have no idea
　　how difficult it is
　　to remember the lines in a play like this
　　let alone to turn those lines
　　into a work of art
　　which this text is without a shadow of doubt
　　Women really do create tremendous difficulties on the stage

they've never understood anything
They don't go to extremes
they don't go to hell—to the hell of the theatre
everything they do is half-hearted
half-heartedness that they understand
but this half-heartedness
is the death of the theatre
But what would a comedy like mine be
without female performers
we need them
If our comedy is to flourish
we need women in our comedy
that's the truth
however bitter it may be
If you only knew what it cost me
to teach my wife the most rudimentary rules of acting
even the most obvious things demand years of martyrdom
on the one hand we need female performers
on the other hand they spell death to the theatre
As far as women are concerned
we mustn't exaggerate our chivalry
or our mendacity
will become too obvious
Just the word Odense
she had to say it eight thousand times
before I was able to accept it
quite softly
Odense
What could be simpler
to say Odense quite softly
took my wife years
before she could say it acceptably
On the other hand we mustn't drive female performers
to extremes
otherwise they'll stab us in the back
they put up with a lot
but there are limits my dear sir
When we utter the word *sea*
we have to know what the sea is
that's self-evident
or the words *rat poison*
whatever that is
it's self-evident
but not for women

They have to be trained for decades and decades
to understand even the simplest thing
And how difficult it is
when the woman in question is one's own wife
whom we have after all taken forever so to speak
Making scenes with women
is a disaster
When we engage a female performer
we engage so to speak a theatrical monkey wrench
and it's always female performers
who kill the theatre
even if we never frankly admit it
because we are too chivalrous to do so
a female tragedienne
has always been an absurdity after all
in view of the fact that a tragedy
in and of itself is nothing more than an insane idea
If we are honest
theatre is itself an absurdity
but if we are honest
we can't put on theatre
neither can we if we are honest
write a play
or act one
if we are honest
we can't do anything
but do away with ourselves
but as we don't do away with ourselves
because we don't want to do away with ourselves
at least until today and not up till now
since then we have not done away with ourselves till today and up
till now
we keep giving the theatre another try
we write for the theatre
we perform in the theatre
even though that is the absurdest thing possible
and the most mendacious
How can an actor play the part of a king
when he doesn't have the faintest idea what a king is
how can an actress play the part of a stable lass
when she doesn't have the faintest idea what a stable lass is
when a nationally recognized actor plays a king
it's insipid
when a nationally recognized actress plays a stable lass

that's even more insipid
but time and again all actors play something
that they cannot be
and that is nothing more than insipid
thus everything in the theatre is insipid my dear sir
Since actors are very stupid people
it is insipidity personified for them to
play Schopenhauer and Kant for example
or when a nationally recognized actor plays Frederick the Great
or when even Voltaire is played by an actor
that's all insipidity
of course I have always been aware
of this fact
An actor's representation is always
a misrepresentation
simply mendacious my dear sir
and for that very reason it is theatre
Representation is mendacity
and represented mendacity is what we love
That's how I've written my comedy
mendacious
that's how we present it
mendacious
and that's how it's received
mendacious
The writer is mendacious
the actors are mendacious
and the audience is mendacious too
and the sum total is one single absurdity
to say nothing of the fact
that we are dealing with a perversity
dating back for millennia
the theatre is a millennial perversity
which humanity is besotted with
and so deeply besotted because
it is so deeply besotted with its mendacity
and nowhere else in this humanity
is mendacity greater and more fascinating
than in the theatre
licking his left index finger and holding it up in the air, after a pause
My finger will not dry in this hall
dampness like this
is poison to the theatre
My words carried in Gaspoltshofen

here everything is dispersed
everything shrivels up
here the most extraordinary things become
dilettantish
Austria
Degenerate
is the right word
Gone to seed
is the right expression
directly to the Landlord
As a matter of fact
I did have an Austrian grandmother
I'll have you know
a great grandmother by the name of Irrsiegler
But that means nothing to you
pensively as if he were drawing something on the floor
Something Tyrolean
in my nature
something perverse too
Austria
grotesque
underendowed
is the right word
mentally incompetent
is the right expression
Mozart Schubert
odious predominance
Believe me
there is nothing about this people
which is engaging anymore
Wherever we go
envy
smallness of mind
xenophobia
hatred of art
Nowhere else is art received
with the same obtuseness
exclaiming
Art, art art
here they do not even know
what that is
The true artist
is dragged down into the mire
but the mendacious good-for-nothing

is loved
they bow and scrape
to the charlatan
directly to the landlord
Landlord of an inn in Utzbach
what an existence
Did you grow up here
or did you marry
into this Utzbach
Landlord
Married into it Herr Bruscon
Bruscon
Married into it
married into it where from
Landlord
From Gaspoltshofen
Bruscon
From Gaspoltshofen
To be honest with you
I was rather taken by Gaspoltshofen
quite different sort of people
quite different conditions
from here in Utzbach
didn't stink of pigs
no pestiferous silos
But why didn't you stay in Gaspoltshofen
You unlucky fellow
after a pause
To come to Utzbach
for the sake of a woman
pause
You'd probably have developed better
in Gaspoltshofen
Who knows
you had no alternative
The female lures the male
from the most beautiful region
into the worst of holes
Everything here is crippling
everything is unappetizing
everything is stunted
The children all have rickety voices
Discouraging

enervating
annihilating
But when did you come here
Landlord
Forty-six
Bruscon
Forty-six
fateful
fateful
Landlord
In Gaspoltshofen
I had no way of making a living
after my father died
Bruscon
No way of making a living
Early loss of his father
asking
And your mother's still alive
Landlord *shakes his head*
Bruscon
What did she die of
Landlord
Of gastronomy
Bruscon
Of gastronomy
Landlord
It wasn't her fault in the least
We were leasing
a lunch counter
Bruscon
exclaiming
A lessee's fate
there is nothing more tragic
than the fate of a lessee
and worst of all the gastronomic fate
A gastronomic lessee
is a misfortune
in any case
Landlord
There were eleven of us
eight brothers and three sisters
in three beds
in a cold and damp cellar

Bruscon
   You had no choice but to
   marry into gastronomy
standing and taking a few steps
directly to the Landlord, touching him with his cane
   It's possible that Utzbach
   was your salvation
Landlord
   Yes
Bruscon
   This awful Utzbach
   in which I would die of Catholic depression
   if I had to spend another day here
   was your salvation
looking around
   This architectural helplessness
   the horror of these walls
   the frightfulness of the ceiling
   the repulsiveness of the doors and windows
   this monument to bad taste
   has provided for your continued existence
sitting again
   we often ask ourselves
   are we
   or is the world mad
pensively
   Innkeeper in Utzbach
   if that isn't lunacy
   complete lunacy
calling into the hall
   The most complete lunacy
   of all times
   He who exists
   has made his peace with existence
   he who lives
   has made his peace with life
   the part we play cannot be so
   preposterous
   that we do not not play it
looking at the windows
   We've brought some curtains
   which completely cover all the windows
   special curtains

we had them made in the Klepper works in Rosenheim
they cost eighty thousand
but without these special curtains
our comedy would be totally impossible
We've also got some special hooks in our luggage
we can nail these special hooks
into any wall
it doesn't matter what sort of wall it is
we can nail them in
Our lights are from a special factory
in Recklinghausen
We have the advantage
of traveling in a single van
and this van is not by any means uncomfortable
looking at the floor
I had originally wanted to go for a walk with Agatha
with Agatha my wife
to stretch our legs so to speak
for an hour or two
but there's simply nowhere to walk here
it's uphill everywhere
and wherever you look it's ugly anyway
And so we thought that we would
simply order frittata soup
and stay in the hotel
But your dining room was closed
and in the beer-garden the stench of the pigs
was intolerable
As if you hadn't known
we were coming today
but you knew perfectly well
The fact that no one opened the door
until we had knocked persistently on it
is a perverse singularity
And when the weather is so sultry
there is a stench of butchery
On the other hand it is advantageous
to stay at an inn
where the butchery is done on the premises
directly to the Landlord
I do not think
that in the circumstances
we can air this room out

if we open the windows
we shall be lost
But when do you feed the pigs
Landlord
At half past five
Bruscon
As usual at half past five
That's no problem
In Mattighofen
because as we were told there'd been a death in the family
the pigs were fed at half past eight
they disrupted everything by grunting
the pigs grunting ruined the whole play
At first we wanted to call a halt
but then we decided
to carry on with the play
The play was ruined right at the climax by the pigs grunting
To be honest with you I didn't care
I didn't have a true sense of mission in Mattighofen
I think the people there only came to our play
to cool off
because it was as sultry as it is here today
We did an abridged version in Mattighofen
Cut the Einstein scene
everything that is said about the atom bomb
in my play
a definitive statement to be sure
we managed without this scene in Mattighofen
by the way I also cut
the scene where Napoleon makes fun of the King of Saxony
however this caused my wife the greatest difficulties
Women are not as flexible as we are
they're dull creatures
Of course that was the great hiatus in my play
but there was terrific applause
we were given a bonus in Mattighofen
a wheel of cheese
but my wife doesn't eat cheese
I myself do not like cheese
and my children are totally opposed to cheese
So we drag this great wheel of cheese around
possibly we'll find someone to take it off our hands
The wheel of cheese weighs forty-three kilograms
It presses heavily on our rear axle

By the way Sarah is driving
because Ferruccio has a broken hand
in Zwicklett
my son plunged from the second floor
on his way to the toilet
fateful slip
could easily have killed him
but my children are very limber
Here the privy's outside as well
I can't ask my wife to go outside to the privy
Please
put two chamber pots in our room
Liver dumpling soup
or frittata soup
that was always the question
till I finally
decided in favor of frittata soup
If we eat liver dumpling soup in the afternoon
we cannot perform in the evening
the stomach uses up all the energy
and leaves the head empty
Your wife was so strangely silent
when she admitted us
She scarcely said "good day"
I know this region is unequalled for unfriendliness
but a short friendly greeting
does the person arriving a lot of good
The further we travel down the Danube
the more unfriendly it becomes
sultry and unfriendly
not to say really misanthropic
In Gallspach we were
enchanted by a little spring
in a shady beer-garden
and wanted to eat some headcheese so to speak
But the waitress
who had come to our table
was cutting her
fingernails
while she was talking to us
And when one of those fingernails
flew into my wife's face
we fled from the inn
If you travel from place to place here

you experience some of the strangest things my dear sir
and at the same time pretty well all the horrors
of Austrian gastronomy
What I found so fascinating in Gaspoltshofen
to be honest with you
was not the audience
not even that we gave an absolutely magnificent performance there
but simply and solely the fact
that we had a white tablecloth
on the table
where in other places it is only filthy sticky plastic rags
on which the meals are served
A journey through this region is anything
but appetizing
And therefore I mostly eat even my frittata soup
with my eyes closed
and actually almost always enjoy it
Oh don't torture me
please go and ask
whether it's possible
for us to have a frittata soup here and now
The soup by which we exist so to speak
exit **Landlord**
Bruscon
    Wheelwright and fire chief
    What funny people there are
    wielding the scepter of power
    the most ridiculous
    brings about the fall of the most sublime
looking around
    Disgusting
    When Agatha sees this
    Nothing but filth and stench
looking along the walls
    and these ugly prints
    they'll all have to go
    I am not going to perform with these prints on the wall
    This hall is a proper spirit-killer
    Rent for the hall
    don't make me laugh
    Bruscon isn't paying any rent for the hall
    for a pigsty like this
turning around and looking at the back of the stage
    Caesar can enter from the back there

but Napoleon cannot enter from down left
that won't work here
But the Caesar-Napoleon scene can't be cut
We might be able to manage without
Hitler
No
not here
no we've got to have Hitler here
looking to the right
Then Sarah enters
and says Ludwig how could you
Ferruccio replies do not insult me
after all I'm not shooting at him
We could leave that out
like everything in fact
concerning love
leave out love
But on the other hand not entirely
Basically everything is equally important
In my *Wheel of History* everything is equally important
The cast didn't put themselves out in Gaspoltshofen
because I said
Gaspoltshofen what cretins
the cretinization of humanity
I shouldn't have said that
it made them play badly right away
worse than ever before
They'll play even worse in Utzbach
if I tell them
what I think about Utzbach
But of course they can see
what Utzbach's like
poor Agatha
on the other hand I don't feel a bit sorry for her
Women *make* a scene
Men *are* the scene
Women make a scene
that's the difficulty
Basically children without talent
that's it
taken nothing in
told them everything
heard nothing
showed them everything

saw nothing
The father can say what he likes
it's no use
The mother spoils everything
that the father has accomplished
looking at the floor of the platform
Feebleminded son
more or less
stupid daughter
looking at the window
wife who constantly thinks she's been slighted
driving me crazy
Product of the proletariat
proletarian product
I after all did not want
to do the tour
I was always against this tour
but because she kept tormenting me
with her good country air
I gave in
Consumptives are difficult people
well-nigh insufferable
despots of the world so to speak
fanatics for perfidy
The good country air
which we shall breathe on our tour
she repeated it over and over again
and really it's nothing but stench
and her condition
has never been as bad as it is now
Even the doctor said
go on tour with your wife
Doctors are all idiots
it's just that we keep control of ourselves
when we are in their clutches
but they are all idiots
Gave in off we went on our tour
disgusting weakness of character on my part
The Wheel of History
more or less
cast before swine
If I had staged it in Cologne
or Bochum as far as I'm concerned

in the Rhineland or the Ruhr
everything would have been better
This way I've ruined it for myself
Always allowing myself to be talked into everything
Utzbach like Butzbach
Half-rotten bed linen
torn plastic curtains
view of the pigsty
If I hadn't seen
the thousands of blood stains on the wall
from the gnats they've slain
they call them midges here
She did have the shivers
Agatha I said
mustn't get sick
here
in this
in this Utzbach
Kiss on the forehead
Nothing we can't handle I said
straightening himself up to his full height as the **Landlord** *enters*
Is it possible
the frittata soup
Landlord
My wife's already seeing to it
Although she's needed to fill sausages
Bruscon
To fill sausages
Landlord
It's blood sausage day today
Bruscon
Blood sausage day
blood sausage day
does that mean something
Landlord
It's the day blood sausages are made
Bruscon
Blood sausage day
Today of all days
is blood sausage day here
Landlord
But it won't take long
to make a frittata soup

Bruscon
  I see
Landlord
  Then Erna is coming
  to sweep up
Bruscon
  Erna is coming
  Erna
  who is Erna
Landlord
  My daughter
Bruscon
  I see
Landlord *having brought in a few armchairs places them at the end of*
  the hall
  On blood sausage day we all have to
  work together
Bruscon
  I see
  so it's not an auspicious day
  for us
Landlord
  For anybody
  On blood sausage day
  we usually have no time
Bruscon
  Usually
  no time
  on blood sausage day
Landlord
  But never mind
Bruscon
  Never mind
  never mind
  Do you have blood sausage day
  every week
Landlord
  Every Tuesday
pulls up a curtain and immediately tears it down and throws it to the
  floor
Bruscon
  But all the curtains are done for
looking up at the ceiling
  The ceiling's all cracks

Landlord
   More than forty years
   since it was painted
Bruscon
   I see
looks at the prints
   and these pictures these landscapes
   they're nothing but ugly stains
   behind glass
   These pictures must come down
   I can't perform under these ugly pictures
looking at one particular print
   Isn't that a picture of Hitler
Landlord
   Certainly it is
Bruscon *inquiringly*
   And has it always hung there
Landlord
   Certainly it has
Bruscon *inquiringly*
   For decades
Landlord
   Certainly
Bruscon
   You have to look very closely indeed
   to see that it is Hitler
   the glass is so filthy
Landlord
   No one's taken umbrage about that
   so far
Bruscon
   No one's taken umbrage
   If you're talking to people from the city
   your speech is more or less educated
   at least you make an effort to that end
   on the one hand that's very commendable
   on the other
   Hitler also appears in my play
   encounters Napoleon and
   has drinks with Roosevelt on the Obersalzberg
   If I don't cut that scene this evening
   Hitler's picture can stay on the wall
   that's not bad at all
   Goethe gets an attack of coughing

and is carried out of the salon by Kierkegaard
after Hitler and Napoleon have entered
Kierkegaard
the great Dane
who wrote *Eitheror*
of course that means nothing to you
sitting down exhausted
When we come to a place
it's a stupid place
when we meet someone
it's someone stupid
talking directly to the Landlord in a whisper
A thoroughly stupid country
populated
by people who are thoroughly stupid
It doesn't matter who we talk to
it turns out
that it's a fool
it doesn't matter who we listen to
it turns out that
it's an illiterate
they're socialists
they claim
and are only national socialists
they're Catholic
they claim
and are only national socialists
they say they're human
and are only idiots
looking round
Austria
Österreich
L'Autriche
It seems to me
as if we're touring
in a cesspool
in the pus-filled boil of Europe
beckoning to the Landlord
whispering in his ear
Why does everything stink round here
What a horrible return
my dear sir
in a normal tone again
At every street corner

there's something to turn your stomach
Where there was once a wood
now there's a gravel pit
where there was once a meadow
there's a cement works
where there was once a human being
there's a nazi
And always on top of everything else
this electrically charged atmosphere of the Lower Alps
in which a sensitive person
is in constant fear
of an apoplectic fit
This tour is proof positive
This country
is not worth the paper
its travel brochures are printed on
exhausted
    Utzbach
    A conspiracy
    against me
    against everything
    that's of any value
exclaiming
    A trap for art dear sir
    a trap for art
directly to the landlord
    Tell me
    do you have blood sausage day every week
Landlord
    Every Tuesday is blood sausage day
Bruscon
    Every Tuesday
Landlord *who has climbed up on to a window sill, to take down a huge*
    cobweb from the window
    Every Tuesday
Bruscon
    Is every day sausage day
Landlord
    Every other day is sausage day
Bruscon
    But Tuesday is always
    blood sausage day
Landlord
    Yes

jumping down from the window sill and throwing the cobweb on to the floor

Bruscon

Every Tuesday is blood sausage day
I should have known that
If I didn't detest
every sort of sausage
except for headcheese

trying to get up but sitting again immediately

Then my limbs suddenly
give way
That confounded Zwicklett
My son could have
plunged to his death
His right arm in a cast
at first I thought
this is a dreadful calamity
but then I saw
that it is only people like that with a crippled right arm
that my son plays
Hitler had a crippled right arm
Nero
as you know
Caesar
even Churchill had a crippled right arm
the so-called great rulers
all had crippled rights arms
On the contrary with his arm in a cast
he plays these so-called great rulers
to even greater perfection
than he did before
These are parts that I wrote
especially for my son
that anti-talent
just like the parts for my daughter
not to mention the parts
which my wife plays
gigantic anti-talentism dear sir
When we write a comedy
and even if it is the so-called world comedy
we have to take full account of the fact
that it will be performed by dilettantes
by anti-talents
that is our lot

The dramatist does well
to be cognizant of the fact
that only anti-talents
will put his play on the stage
even if they are the greatest and most famous actors
they are anti-talents
everyone who treads the boards
is an anti-talent
and the more grand they appear
and the more famous they are
the more disgusting is their anti-talent
A talented actor
is as rare as an arsehole in a face
That was an observation made by Pirandello
or perhaps I made it myself
Pirandello did make such observations
but I myself have constantly made such observations
most of the time I don't know
did *I* make that observation
or did Pirandello make it
I don't know
So I have to take it as a special honor
that you take time for me
on blood sausage day of all days
when I assume you are certainly needed at the butcher's
to fill the blood sausages
Sarah *and* **Ferruccio** *(with his right hand in a cast) enter with a large*
crate
Bruscon
Put the crate over here
here
they carry the crate to the spot where Bruscon wants it placed
I said here
pointing with his cane
Here
Not there for heaven's sake
the crate is picked up and put down again
Bruscon
Here
put the crate down here
the crate here
here
here where I told you
Landlord *comes up onto the platform and helps to carry the crate*

Bruscon
  But I said
  here
they put the crate down
Bruscon *touching the crate*
  But the crate is all damp
  That will spoil the masks
  this sultry
  this humid sultry weather
  of course it has to hurt the masks
Ferruccio *tries to open the lid of the crate but he cannot because his*
  hand is in a cast
Bruscon
  Ah landlord if you please
  you unlock the crate would you
  my son is a cripple
  he is incapable
  of unlocking the crate
  Now the fool
  is a cripple as well
Landlord *unlocks the crate*
Bruscon *to Sarah*
  But don't you see
  I'm bathed in sweat
  really can't you see that my child
Sarah *wipes the sweat from her father's forehead with a large handke*
Landlord *opens the crate up all the way*
Bruscon
  But why did you keep me waiting
  here so long
  Left me sitting here alone
  in this dreadful hall
  where I'll catch a fatal disease
  forsaken by everyone
  I sit here
  in this hard chair
  with only the landlord for company
to the Landlord
  There you see
  that's what you can expect from your children
  children you fathered
  and coddled for decades
  that they forsake you
to Ferruccio

That ridiculous fracture
that's no excuse
for total incompetence
to the Landlord
　　At least I still have
　　a drop of Italian blood in me
　　a passion for art
looking into the open crate
　　a touch of genius my dear sir
　　but there's nothing Italian left
　　in these children
　　My grandfather on my mother's side
　　let me tell you
　　an emigrant's fate
　　from Bergamo across the Alps
　　to Kiel
　　on the Baltic
　　a railroad laborer's fate
　　building the line from Hamburg to Copenhagen my dear sir
　　The great Bruscon
　　never denied his roots
to Sarah
　　Take them off for me
stretching his legs out
　　I want you to take my shoes off
　　Everything hurts
　　everything
　　I'm nothing but a man of sorrows
Sarah *takes his shoes off, he stretches his legs as far as possible,*
　　wiggles his toes
Bruscon
　　Do it the way you did in Gaspoltshofen
peering into the crate
　　The way you did in Gaspoltshofen my child
　　from top to bottom
　　from bottom to top
　　the way you did in Gaspoltshofen my child
Sarah *massages the soles of her father's feet*
　　Yes that's the way
Ferruccio *suddenly takes the mask of Caesar out of the crate and*
　　holds it in front of the **Landlord's** *face.*
Bruscon *furious*
　　What on earth are you doing
　　Put the mask back into the crate at once

at once back into the crate
inadvertently kicking **Sarah** *in the face with his feet*
    Put the mask back in the crate at once
    What are you thinking of
    it's abominable
    holding Caesar's mask up to people of that ilk
    an unworthy creature
    a landlord
    an enemy of the arts
    a hater of the theatre
    what impudence
    an abomination
Ferruccio *puts the mask back into the crate*
Bruscon
    Close the crate
    close it
    close the crate again
Ferruccio *closes the lid of the crate*
Bruscon *to the landlord*
    What are you standing around for
    why are you staring at me
    who do you think
    you are
    Oh what's the use
stretching out his legs
Landlord *makes to exit*
Bruscon
    No no
    stay here
    everything gets on my nerves here
    that's it
    in this
    in this
Sarah *massages the soles of his feet again*
Bruscon
    in this
Landlord
    Utzbach
Bruscon
    in this Utzbach
    like Butzbach
to the Landlord
    Forgive me
    I don't as a rule

I never do as a rule
but this sultriness
to Sarah
Would you *mind* helping me
off with my coat
rises, **Sarah** *helps him out of his topcoat*
Bruscon
Victims of our passion
we all are
no matter what we do
we are the victims of our passion
Sarah *takes his topcoat and gives it to* **Ferruccio** *who passes it to the*
  Landlord *in his turn, who puts it over his arm.*
Bruscon
We are at death's door
and behave as though
we were immortal
we've already reached the end
and act as if
it could go on and on like this
dropping into the armchair
Sarah my child
you must stand by me
all the more so
when it's hell
come here
pulling her to him and kissing her on the forehead
You've learned nothing
but I love you
more than anything
suddenly curious
And what about mother
has she memorized her lines
Sarah *nods*
Bruscon
Your mother
is an anti-talent
but for that very reason
I took her
and do you know where
Sarah
On the Atlantic coast
Bruscon
Exactly

on the Atlantic coast
it was in Le Havre
Funny that all these coastal towns
have always meant so much to me
Le Havre Ostend
Kiel my child
but also Palermo
to Ferruccio
Tonight you'll play Caesar
slightly muted you understand
slightly muted
Hitler somewhat more cheerful than usual
not as melancholy as in Gaspoltshofen
Hitler was not a melancholy man
I need Churchill to show a little more sensuality
you understand
a little more sensuality
to Sarah
Memorized it you say
your mother has memorized her lines
and you went through them with her
Sarah *nods*
Bruscon
Probably
wasn't any good again
She has never been any good
she never understood
to think of all that I have tried to teach her
she didn't understand a thing
But she brought a beautiful child into the world
you
drawing Sarah toward him and kissing her on the forehead again to
Ferruccio
Our bourgeois
At bottom you were not made for the theatre
I'm at my wits end
I often say to myself
that's our son
who cannot appreciate poetry
who has no inkling of
imagination
no inkling of the spirit
no inkling of the creative
beckoning to him

Come here
I didn't mean it that way
Ferruccio *goes to his father*
Bruscon
You are my greatest disappointment
you know that
but you have never disappointed me
No one is as useful to me
exit **Landlord**
Bruscon *calling after him*
You could serve
the frittata soup my dear sir
I would like to ask for a piping *hot* soup
usually it comes to the table lukewarm
looks around
That's the price we pay
that's what we get for
listening to your mother
and going on tour
because of her precious pulmonary lobes
Horrid isn't it
Utzbach that's what this place is called
Utzbach like Butzbach
hugging Sarah
The world is cruel my child
and spares no one
not a single person
nothing
everything is destroyed by it
Whoever thinks
he can escape
is caught up with immediately
everyone's destination
is misfortune
and the end
Look at this frightful hall
that's just what I needed
And this seedy landlord
who exudes such a noisome odor
even wants to charge me rent for the hall
And the fire chief
will not allow
the emergency exit light to be switched off
but I'm not going to perform

I said
unless the emergency exit light is extinguished
total darkness I said
I'm not going to have my comedy ruined in this
awful Utzbach place
These people don't even deserve
to have you come to their village at all
let alone
have a theatre company play here
and the great Bruscon into the bargain
directly to Sarah
Have you mended the wig
Sarah
Yes
Bruscon *to Ferruccio*
And you
have you patched the shoes
Ferruccio
Yes
Bruscon
Our intensity
our travel intensity I mean
must not flag
of course tonight we shall play
the *whole* comedy
I shall cut nothing
just because we are where we are
to Sarah
Is she still coughing your mother
Sarah
She's still coughing
she even coughed while she was doing her lines
Bruscon
I thought as much
I thought she'd cough her lines away
didn't she take any cough medication
Sarah
Oh yes she did
Bruscon
Why is she coughing then
Such beautiful lines
such a magnificent passage
and she coughs it all away

But we must not make peace with
mediocrity
That's what's proletarian about her
the way she destroys whatever is magnificent
even if it's only by coughing
Your mother is a proletarian
But I love her
that's the truth
she irritates me all the time
but I love her
Did she speak the passage *softly*
as I told her to
Sarah *nods*
Bruscon
What do you mean
did she not
did she not start the passage softly
as I directed
She's not to speak the passage
the way she did in Gaspoltshofen
that was enough to try the patience of Job
I know
the two of you are in cahoots
You stand by me
but you make allowances for your mother's
artistic blunders
her artistic incompetence
you can still hear even today
in every sentence that comes out of her mouth
that her father was a bricklayer
It's not a disgrace to be a bricklayer
but still to notice the bricklayer
who was her father
in every sentence even to this day
that's insidious
But the fact is
we can always tell with any actor
no matter who it is
what his father was
that's what's depressing my child
Unfortunately no one can tell from the two of you
that your father is Bruscon
the great nationally recognized actor

the greatest nationally recognized actor that there ever was
stretching his legs out, **Sarah** *massages the soles of his feet*—**Ferruccio**
stands behind Bruscon and makes massaging movements on his
shoulders
Bruscon
You two
are born massage artists
You ought to have been masseurs
you'd have gone far if you had been
stretching his legs out still further
Massage yes
acting no
Humanity doesn't have the least idea
what that is
an excellent massage
It was *I* of course who taught you how to massage
Your mother was incompetent as a masseuse too
Slowly and very gently
closing his eyes
There is nothing more necessary than a good massage
before going on
stimulates the imagination
conjures up all the good spirits
makes art possible
the highest art
Landlord *and* **Landlord's Wife** *enter bringing the frittata soup*
Bruscon
What an aroma
to Sarah
Help me up
Sarah *helps him up*
Landlord *and* **Landlord's Wife** *put the plates on the table and pour out*
the frittata soup
Bruscon
Are you sure it's really hot
Landlord
The soup is piping hot
Bruscon
Frittata soup children
Now give your poor frail father a hand
to get to the table
Ferruccio *and* **Sarah** *take their father between them and lead him to*
the table
Erna *enters with a yard broom*

Bruscon
  Nobody knows where
  frittata soup comes from
  Probably from Bohemia
Sarah *pushes an armchair behind Bruscon*
Bruscon *sitting down*
  But it doesn't matter
  where it comes from
  frittata soup
Madame Bruscon *enters in a quilted dressing gown*
Sarah *to Bruscon*
  Mother's here
Bruscon
  What did you say
Sarah
  Mother is here
  our mother is here
Bruscon
  Where is she
Sarah
  There
Bruscon
  There, there
takes a spoonful of soup
  I don't see her
Sarah
  There's mother
  there
Bruscon *looking up*
  Oh yes you
taking a spoonful of soup
  Excellent soup
  quite excellent frittata soup
  But do sit down everybody
  do sit down
all sit except the mother
Bruscon *barking at the mother*
  Come on sit down
  why are you standing there
  what on earth are you waiting for
Madame Bruscon *sits down opposite Bruscon*
Bruscon *after a pause*
  You coughed the passage away
  is that true

you're surely not serious
coughing the passage away
as Sarah informs me
that's a nice prospect for tonight
tonight of all nights
when I intended
to give a gala performance more or less
spooning his soup
more or less
you heard me right
a gala performance
exeunt **Landlord** *and* **Landlord's Wife**
in this charming place
The children wanted to take a walk to the pond
they followed a signpost
which said *To the Pond*
but they ended up in a rubbish dump
pause
Utzbach
Utzbach like Butzbach
roughly to Madame Bruscon
Go on eat
we haven't had such a good soup
for a long time
such a good frittata soup
Erna *starts sweeping furiously and stirs up enormous amounts of dust*
Everyone starts coughing

Scene Two

Half an hour later
While **Ferruccio** *is standing on a ladder, putting up the curtain*
Bruscon *sitting in an armchair, to* **Sarah** *who is kneeling down in front*
of him
Softly my child

you know that
I don't like you
to say these lines too loud
Nowadays people bawl their parts in comedies
It doesn't matter where we go
all we hear is bawling
And not only in the provinces
even in the great houses people bawl nowadays
Very softly in this passage you hear
you yourself think
that no one can hear you
but they have to hear you
you speak so softly that you think
you can't be heard
and you speak very clearly
demonstrating
When beauty doth elude us evermore
and sickness of the spirit seize our soul
and leave us naked to our very core
You see that's how it goes
you speak so softly that you think
no one at all can hear you
but that's a mistake
The person who speaks perfectly is heard
even if he himself speaks so softly
that he thinks he can't be heard
Sarah
When beauty doth elude us evermore
and sickness of the spirit seize our soul
and leave us naked
Bruscon
Not quite
once again
Unaffected on the one hand
the highest artistic penetration on the other
you know
what I mean
Well
Sarah
When beauty doth elude us
Bruscon
Oh no
can't you understand

softly
Unaffected on the one hand
highest artistic penetration on the other
Sarah
When beauty doth elude us evermore
and sickness
Bruscon *motions to her to stop*
What is lacking here
is the devotion
with which you must speak those lines
you lack devotion
you must speak this in the most devout way too
Listen
When beauty doth elude us evermore
and sickness
lightly softly lightly
devoutly my child
Well
Sarah
When beauty doth elude us evermore
Bruscon *interrupting*
This is simply impossible
as though you had never learned
there is no difference between you
and the dilettantism which is rampant
everywhere today
People simply cannot speak anymore
Even in our national theatres
no one can speak anymore
In the most famous theatres in Germany
the way people speak today
is enough to frighten a pig
Perhaps the part is too much for you after all
Sometimes I think you take
after your mother completely
Sarah *stands up*
Bruscon
You will come to me after the performance
and we'll rehearse this passage
and if it's two in the morning
No excuse
I always thought
that I was an excellent teacher
but that was an erroneous assumption

I don't expect any flights of genius from Ferruccio
but from you my child
Come here
give me your hand
Sarah *gives him her hand*
Bruscon
  What is your father
  what is your father
Sarah
  Herr Bruscon
Bruscon *pushing her away*
  Impudent girl
  how dare you
  This impertinence
  will cost you dearly
  Come here
  here I said
Sarah *goes to him*
Bruscon
  I won't abide any argument
  or any insubordination
taking her hand and pressing it so hard that it hurts her
  Now then what is your father
  tell me what your father is
Ferruccio *who has been watching the scene*
  Tell him what he is
Bruscon *to Ferruccio*
  You keep quiet
  you ne'er-do-well
  anti-talent
  Ferruccio
  because I am an admirer of Busoni
  but you do no honor
  to Busoni's genius
pressing Sarah's hand even more strongly
  Well then
  what is your father
Sarah *reluctantly*
  The greatest actor
  of all times
Bruscon *pushing her away so that she stumbles*
  Well at last
  That's what I wanted to hear
  Because so far today

no one has said that to me yet
Running away when the chips are down
that's what you all do
Come here
You're to come here
Your father orders you
to come here
Sarah *goes to him*
Bruscon *taking her hand*
Since it didn't
occur to *you*
to tell me
who I am
it has to be wrung from you
I have no other choice my child
We lead a desperate life
a frightful existence
Besides we also have
a sick stupid mother
who has taken refuge in hypochondria
And who coughs her lines away
A disaster
if the fire chief
insists on the law
and does not allow
total darkness in my comedy
Everywhere else it was the easiest thing in the world
here everything is as complicated as it can be
As though here in Utzbach
we had fallen into a trap
to Ferruccio
Have you sewed up the hole
Ferruccio
I have
Bruscon
It had to be velvet
and we're still all moaning and groaning because of it
When it could have been linen
In fact linen would have been better
linen opens more easily
closes more easily
No it had to be velvet
That's your mother's proletarian megalomania
She always suffered from it

a mania for profligacy
If I'd had my way
the costumes would have cost a third of what they did
no she wanted silk for everything
Artificial silk I said
silk she said
linen I said
velvet she said
The proletarians demand luxury
that's it
that's it
that's what brings us to the verge of ruin
When the proletarians go one better
they go the whole hog
Our sort are content with a simple meal
they have to order the most expensive dish
we ask for simple chicken
they order Peking duck
we travel coach
they travel first class
we take a trip
if we ever do take one
to Merano at best or to the mountains
they go to the Seychelles
But of course I have her under my thumb
your mother
she would have put you into silk and satin
from your earliest childhood
cotton was as good
you can thank me that you grew up in cotton
if your mother had had her way
the daughter of a bricklayer
she would have spoiled you to death
from your earliest days
Ever since the proletarians have been ruling the world
the world has been regressing
they promised progress
but in truth it's regressing
no proof whatsoever is needed
just common sense
an open eye so to speak
Now so-called socialism
is presenting us with the bill
the coffers are empty

Europe is done for
It will take a hundred years
before what they've ruined
is restored
What hurts me most
is the fact
that the proletarians have also
destroyed the theatre
that's the truth
But why am I talking to you
who have never yet understood
what I was talking about
to Ferruccio
We'll have a lighting rehearsal at six
Green light from above
slowly onto Churchill's face
not like Gaspoltshofen
where no light at all fell on Churchill's face
to Sarah
And as Lady Churchill
you will wear the red shoes
You think I never notice anything
in Gaspoltshofen you were wearing the black ones
Lady Churchill in my comedy
wears red shoes not black
It is of the utmost importance
that she should wear red shoes
and not black ones
I won't stand for underhandedness
Lady Churchill wears red shoes
Metternich's mistress wears the black ones
Even if *you* don't understand why
I know why
that's sufficient
How about bringing me something to drink
I'm dying of thirst here
while your mother
looking up to the ceiling
is taking it easy up there
pretending to have caught a chill
I am dying of thirst down here
Perhaps they have *Perrier* here
looking up at the ceiling again
Sheer underhandedness

to keep faking illnesses
which she simply doesn't have
I don't need a doctor
to tell me that she is
completely healthy
Hysterical that's what it is
pretending to have a cough
making a fuss about asthma
your mother has an immense reservoir
of symptoms of illness
suddenly to Sarah
    Why are you still standing there
    I said *Perrier*
    or *Apollinaris*
    but I'm sure they don't have that
    here
    in Utzbach
exit **Sarah**
Bruscon *to Ferruccio*
    Your mother
    invests her whole talent
    in her pretended illnesses
    instead of in the art of acting
    I know
    that she hates my comedy
    she hates everything about me
    everything spiritual at any rate
    Just be thankful that you have me
    and that you needn't suffocate in a marriage
    That you are artists
    or at least have the appearance of being
    artists
    of course precious few have the faintest idea what that means
    artistes
    if the expression were not so repellent
    I'd use it more often
    but it disgusts me
Ferruccio *having finished hanging the curtain jumps down from the
    ladder*
Bruscon
    Limber
    that's what you have always been
    I don't know where you get it from
    Your mother is stiff

and I am clumsy
you have always been limber
And yet
up till now
I have never broken any bones
Your mother now
she has always been fracture-prone
Landlord *and* **Landlord's Wife** *enter carrying the laundry basket and*
   put it down
Bruscon
   Would you mind very much
   putting the basket over there
pointing with his cane
Landlord *and* **Landlord's Wife** *do as Bruscon tells them*
Bruscon
   There
   yes there
   no there
   there
   that's it
   there
   there
Landlord *and* **Landlord's Wife** *put the basket down*
Bruscon
   This sultriness
   This sultriness on the one hand
   and this feeling
   that I shall freeze to death here
   on the other
to the Landlord
   Have you been to see the fire chief yet
Landlord
   No not yet
Bruscon
   Why in heaven's name not
   When I tell you
   that the emergency exit light is the most important thing
   my comedy can't take an emergency exit light
   do you understand me
   total darkness my dear sir
   tell the fire chief that
   your wheelwright
   now don't misunderstand me
   this isn't meant to be a threat

we shall not perform
if the emergency exit light is not switched off
exclaiming
   This is really ridiculous
   to insist on the emergency exit light
   totally ridiculous
   Now for heaven's sake go
   and say that I sent you
   and that this is absolutely
   the most important thing
to Sarah who has entered carrying a glass of water
   Isn't that right Sarah
to Ferruccio
   Isn't that right my son
to the Landlord
   We shall not perform
   if the emergency exit light is not switched off
   Now be off with you
   we are wasting too much time
to the Landlord's Wife
   What's the word on supper
   Hot supper of course
   An opulent supper theatre style
   What delicacies can you recommend
Landlord's Wife
   Brisket of beef Czech style
   Dumplings and steak salad
Bruscon
   Dumplings and steak salad
   Brisket of beef
   Czech style
   You mean with horseradish
   But it is possible too
   that I am not yet ready to make a decision
   Is it true
   that one of your daughter's eyes is weak
Landlord's Wife
   She has glaucoma
Bruscon
   She has glaucoma the child does
   she'll have to have an operation
Landlord's Wife
   The doctor said
   she would have to have an operation

Bruscon
    You have to operate for glaucoma
    But she's a great help to you
    your daughter in the kitchen isn't she
Landlord's Wife
    I guess so
Bruscon
    A pretty child
    a pity that she has glaucoma
to Ferruccio
    Draw the curtain
exeunt **Landlord** *and* **Landlord's Wife**
Bruscon
    Open it
Ferruccio *draws the curtain*
Bruscon *to Sarah*
    Go and stand behind the curtain
    I want to see the effect
    when you stand behind the curtain
    and the curtain opens
    We didn't even rehearse the curtain
    in Gaspoltshofen
Sarah *goes behind the curtain with the glass of water*
Ferruccio *draws the curtain*
Bruscon
    Yes
    see how easy it is
    not jerkily like Mattighofen
    slow
    but not *too* slow
to Ferruccio
    Close it
    and draw it again
Ferruccio *closes the curtain and draws it again, while* **Sarah** *remains*
        standing picking her nose
Bruscon
    Well done
    Close it
Ferruccio *closes the curtain*
Bruscon
    Open it
Ferruccio *opens the curtain*
Bruscon *pensively*
    How would it be

if Lady Churchill picked her nose
when the curtain rises
No
I'm not joking
Because you were picking your nose my child
it was only an idea
a silly idea it's true
it's true a silly idea
We have all sorts of ideas
but they are mostly silly
to Ferruccio
Close the curtain again
Ferruccio *closes the curtain again*
Bruscon
Open it again
a bit faster than before
but not *too* fast
Ferruccio *opens the curtain*
Sarah *sticks her tongue out at Bruscon*
Bruscon *to Sarah*
You think
I don't notice you
sticking your tongue out at me
A cheap effect
to annoy your father
I shall ignore it
to Ferruccio
All right
close the curtain again
so that I don't have to look
at this ugly child any longer
collapsing exhausted into the armchair
Ferruccio *closes the curtain*
Bruscon *after a pause shouting angrily*
Perrier
Sarah *goes to Bruscon with the glass of water*
Bruscon *takes a drink realizes that it is ordinary tap water which
Sarah has brought and spits it out*
Ordinary water
tap water
here in Utzbach
here where everything is contaminated
where everything is an open sewer
pushing Sarah away with the water

the glass falls to the floor
   I said *Perrier*
   mineral water
   sealed mineral water
   And you take it upon yourself
   to give your father ordinary and what's more brackish
   Utzbach water
   What an impertinence
Sarah *picks up the pieces of glass*
Bruscon
   At least you could have brought beer
   But no
   I'd kill my comedy
   if I were to drink a single drop of beer
   I wouldn't be able to speak a single sentence
to Ferruccio
   Ferruccio
   listen carefully
   You are to go into the village
   and bring me three or four bottles of mineral water
   in a general store
   I should think
   they would have some mineral water in stock
   if not
   you must drive to Gaspoltshofen
   and bring me a few bottles of *Perrier*
   They had *Perrier* in Gaspoltshofen
   Now go along
   Meanwhile Sarah and I will rehearse
   the encounter between Metternich and Napoleon
   on Zanzibar
barking at Ferruccio
   Go on off with you
Ferruccio *exits*
Bruscon *drawing Sarah to him*
   How lovely my child
   to be alone with you
   when these terrible people
   are all away
takes a handkerchief from the pocket of his coat
Sarah *mops his brow*
   I'm worried about my heart
   my child
   it's been worrying me all this time

Your mother insists
that she suffers with her heart
but I really *do*
stroking Sarah's hand
When we finally get to Rouen
you shall have the evening gown
that you want
Rouen
a culmination
Just between the two of us
I am a classic writer
soon what has been our secret
up to now
will be known to the whole world
My God
what is Goethe my child
Do you realize
that I worked for eight months
on the Metternich scene alone
Agatha never understood
why I more or less locked myself up in my room
for eight months
denied myself to her for that time my child
Eight months for the Metternich scene alone
High art
is a terrible ordeal my child
Ferruccio *enters with two bottles of* Perrier
Bruscon *pushing Sarah away*
What's the meaning of this
Ferruccio *opens a bottle and pours out a glass*
Bruscon
Where
did you get those bottles
Ferruccio
From the landlord's wife
Bruscon
From the landlord's wife
Nonsense
Ferruccio
From the landlord's wife
Bruscon *barking at Sarah*
Impudence
bringing me ordinary water
when they even had *Perrier* here

taking a full glass from Ferruccio and draining it
What bliss
ordering Ferruccio to fill a second glass
I think there's a thunderstorm
brewing
Perrier
the truth is
I hate mineral water
It's delicious
but I hate mineral water
I sacrificed my passion for alcohol
to high art
not a drop of wine for thirty years
hardly a glass of beer
Crazy
if not insane
a completely senseless renunciation
High art
or alcoholism
I've chosen high art
to Sarah
You'll pay for it my child
bringing me
lukewarm Utzbach sewer water
when there was *Perrier* to be had here
has Ferruccio fill him a third glass
I could even go so far as to say
it's champagne
to Sarah
you're in cahoots
with your mother
I have no time
for jokes
that could in some circumstances be fatal
go and practice your monologue
You are the very weakest point
in my comedy
Get out of my sight
chasing her out with his cane
to Ferruccio
How lovely
to be alone with you at last
when all of those who make us despair
bring us to the edge of madness

have gone to hell
My daughter
grows more and more
like her mother
I see it quite clearly
more and more like her
I've always been afraid of that
that she would grow like the woman who bore her
Really Ferruccio
we've nothing to laugh about
stand over there
motioning with his cane to the place where Ferruccio is to stand
Ferruccio *stands there*
Bruscon
Yes there
It always bothers me
when you bow too low
when Napoleon enters
after all you are the King of Saxony
don't forget that
All right please do the bow
Ferruccio *bows*
Bruscon
Yes
Bow yes
but not
obsequiously
royally more or less
leaning forward so that he can see Ferruccio better
Ferruccio *bows*
Bruscon
Very good
quite excellent
Today we'll play Verdi
between acts
not Mozart
Mozart no
have you checked the equipment
Ferruccio *fetches a tape deck and puts it on the table*
Bruscon
Verdi
not Mozart
Mozart here in Utzbach
would be insipid

Ferruccio *plays a few bars*
Bruscon *listening attentively*
  Enough
Ferruccio *turns the tape deck off*
Bruscon
  I hate this music
  I hate music altogether
  in the theatre
  if it isn't opera
  But people have to have music
  between acts
  there's nothing else for it
  Once again
Ferruccio *plays a few bars*
Bruscon
  Bad music
  Verdi well what do you expect
  I can't even stand Mozart anymore
  Turn it off
Ferruccio *turns off the music*
Bruscon
  People don't even know
  what they are listening to
  it just has to be music
  it doesn't matter what it is
  people's stupidity
  has already reached the point
  that they can't be without music
  for even a minute
  Music used to interest me
  now it doesn't any more
  I am more interested
  in silence
  and in the art of words naturally
  in words
  and in the silence in between
  that's it
standing up with difficulty and telling Ferruccio to help him to the rar
pointing with his cane
  These antlers
  these pictures
  must all go
  The walls must be bare
  the walls must be bare

I have always insisted on playing between bare walls
The lack of taste in the country
is without parallel
I didn't pay any rent for the hall in Gaspoltshofen
Here I'm supposed to pay rent for the hall
this disgusting landlord
this disgusting landlord's wife
The landlord
has a wicked case of halitosis
taking a few steps to the right
A nightmare
walking forward and speaking into the hall
Lörrach will fall
taking a few steps to the left and speaking into the hall
And you speak of coal from the Ruhr
Mr. President
going back to the center of the platform
Before swine
In the country
every intellectual product
is cast before swine
I wouldn't even want to be buried
in the country
And yet people find it irresistible
this hypocritical society
sitting again in the armchair
A certain theatrical talent
even as a child
Ferruccio *starts to take the antlers down from the walls as well as the*
picture which is between each pair
Bruscon
Began to be interested in classical literature in earnest
when I was seventeen
thirsty for the spiritual
for the creative
holding up the glass that **Ferruccio** *pours out for him, he drains it*
Take down all the antlers
and all these tasteless landscapes and
portraits
except for the very last one there
do you see
that one
Ferruccio
Not this one

Bruscon
Not that one
That's Hitler
can't you see
Hitler
Ferruccio
You think
that's Hitler
Bruscon
Don't you think so
Ferruccio
I don't know
Bruscon
It's Hitler
All the male portraits here
are of Hitler
all men here are Hitler
I think
we should keep the picture there
as a visual aid so to speak
do you understand me
everyone here is Hitler
Ferruccio *shakes his head*
Bruscon
Even back then the first steps so to speak
into the world of the spirit
at seventeen
earlier still
into the spiritual world of the drama
We mustn't turn tail
never turn tail
looking into the hall and exclaiming
Revenge on you prince
to himself
Very bad
ham
ham
very bad
depressingly bad
shouting
Disastrous relations
between you and the House of Rohan
to himself, as though he were ashamed in front of Ferruccio
I should have left that out

I've shown myself up
unbelievably bad
Suddenly in our declining years
we relapse into
dilettantism
speaking into the hall
Your Majesty
how cruel
but naturally the people
always end up as the worst of fools
to himself
No strength left
In Gaspoltshofen I spoke every line
with such ease
I find it hard here
every word like granite
forces everything to the ground
impossible to think
suddenly to Ferruccio
Did you really pack
my linen cap
I couldn't find it
Ferruccio *who has climbed up the ladder again to straighten the*
curtain
In your coat pocket
Bruscon
In my coat pocket
feeling in his coat pocket
So it is
putting his linen cap on
to Ferruccio
As far as art is concerned
we have never needed
the female sex
on the contrary
they always prevent us
from blossoming
Where would we be today
without them
The whole time I just pretended to myself
that a tour like this
was something
it is nothing but depression
to himself

Devastating
to Ferruccio
Women have no concept of art
women have no idea of anything
philosophical
that's the trouble
they lack a philosophical brain
they try all right
but it's no use
can't be taken seriously
People say that women
are advancing today
sure they are advancing toward disaster
Soon the female will have to declare bankruptcy
I suspect
the world of feeling
just another lie
suddenly
Can you imagine
discussing Schopenhauer
with your mother
We have never been able to
Complete birdbrains
or Montaigne
Then when they don't understand
they turn it all into a joke
The linen cap
sticks to my head
as though I had glued it on
no effect
ineffective
completely ineffective
If it were that easy
Recalcitrance
She drinks peppermint tea
has her feet rubbed with camomile
Dares
to contradict me about Metternich
Refused to polish my shoes
in Gaspoltshofen
calling to Ferruccio
Come here
Ferruccio *jumps down from the ladder and stands in front of Bruscon*

Bruscon
    Only an educated human being
    is a human being
    that is in my understanding
    not in everyone's
    why don't you read
    what I give you to read
    why don't you think
    what ought to be thought
    Swear to me
    that from this day on you will read
    what I order you to
    that you will think
    what I tell you to
    swear
    I'm in earnest about you
    in earnest and caring
    This place of horror
    is a place for swearing oaths
    Will you swear it
    Swear
    Schopenhauer
    Spinoza
suddenly angry
    Oh never mind
    it's all pointless
    I made you swear once before in Osnabrück
    and nothing came of it
Ferruccio *starts to climb the ladder again*
Bruscon *barking at him*
    Up the ladder yes
    to the windows yes
    chauffeuring
exclaiming
    You idiot handyman
    Go on
    get on with it
Ferruccio *climbs the ladder*
Bruscon *to himself*
    I wanted a genius
    and I have a good man
    Nothing is more dangerous
    than good people

Ferruccio *tugs at the curtain*
Bruscon *to himself*
    Curtain puller
    string-puller of stupidity
Ferruccio *jumps down from the ladder and takes more antlers and*
    pictures off the walls
Bruscon *to himself*
    Almost nothing
    of me
    in this person
looking at the floor
    Pay rent for the hall
    Do they think I'm crazy
    Two hundred and thirty inhabitants
    that won't even cover
    expenses
    But things have been worse
    In Merano
    there weren't even three people there
    only a cripple
    who had himself wheeled into the front row
    by the cloakroom attendant
    The only time
    we canceled
    Rent for the hall
    In Gaspoltshofen we could
    have done another performance
    Booked into Utzbach
    crazy
    If I myself in person
calling to Ferruccio
    What do you think
    if I myself in person so to speak
    go and see the fire chief
    about the emergency exit light
    There's no point in trifling with the authorities
    something quite trivial
    can end up
    as an affair of state
    I'm too old for that
    and too feeble
    to take on the government
    A fire chief has it in his power
    to destroy me

these creatures are omnipotent
What do you think
should I go
Ferruccio *shrugs his shoulders*
Bruscon
Don't get involved with the government
that's what your grandfather always said
Landlord *appears in the doorway*
Bruscon *to himself*
That disgusting person
to the landlord
Well what's happened
what's happened about the emergency exit light
what does the fire chief say
Landlord *goes to the podium*
Bruscon
What does he say
the fire chief
Landlord
He's not at home
Bruscon
Nonsense
He's just pretending to be out
You're probably in cahoots
with the fire chief
Not at home
where's he supposed to be
around here
where can he have gone
round here
Landlord
He's driven over to Gallspach
Bruscon
Why didn't you say so
straightaway
Why didn't you say straightaway
that's he's gone to Gallspach
And when will he be back
Landlord
At six
Bruscon
If he comes back at six
then you go to him at six
and tell him

I insist
that the emergency exit light be extinguished
in the last scene
calling into the hall
Behold mankind annihilated
to the Landlord
The crucial sentence
before it is totally dark
Lady Churchill leaves her husband Winston
and Stalin retracts his signature
then it must be perfectly dark
do you understand
And there's something else
your daughter only stirred up dust
she didn't clean
on these window sills
there lies the dust of ages
If you will bring me a bucket of hot water
we'll scrub everything ourselves
we aren't fussy
but where there's dust
it's simply impossible to speak
indicating with his cane that the Landlord
should leave
Now go
we're busy with our dramaturgy at the moment
exit **Landlord**
Bruscon *to Ferruccio*
We underestimate the stupidity
of these people
we think *they* understand
because *we* understand
Wrong
they don't understand anything
In Utzbach it won't even cover our food
Where we have the greatest difficulties
we earn the least
Where everything goes well
it's a sell-out
it's always the same
But after all we perform
for ourselves
to hone our skills
not for this country rabble

ruminatively to himself
  In Gaspoltshofen
  no rent for the hall
  in Gallspach
  no rent for the hall
  in Ried im Innkreis
  no rent for the hall
  only here in this
  in this Utzbach
Ferruccio *has taken down all the pictures and the antlers and is*
  standing in front of the heap
Bruscon
  Take it out
  take all that trash out
  out with it
Ferruccio *gathers up what he can and exits with it*
Bruscon
  It would be better to give
  an evening of violin
  a small violin
  under one's arm
  nothing else
  musicians
  have hit the jackpot
  Acting is a lot of trouble
  everything about it
  repulsive
  just a violin
  nothing else
  we don't even need
  a woman for that
  only a good ear
  and a certain manual dexterity
Ferruccio *enters and collects another heap of antlers and pictures and*
  carries them out
Bruscon *to himself*
  But the simple
  has never attracted me
  Always lived by swimming against the stream
  by the mechanism of counteraction
looking at the floor
  Just a violin
Ferruccio *enters with a bucket of hot water and a rag and wipes all the*
  window sills one after another

Bruscon
 That should be
 woman's work
 woman's work absolutely
 But they shirk it
looking up at the ceiling of the hall
 Lying in bed
 and indulging in *dolce far niente*
 pondering imaginary problems
 feet sticking in a camomile brew
 lolling at the window
to Ferruccio
 Today your mother has a cough
 tomorrow a sore throat
 the day after tomorrow a cough again etcetera
looking at the floor
 sickness fetishism
to Ferruccio commandingly
 Come here come here
Ferruccio *goes at once to Bruscon with the bucket and the rag*
Bruscon *lifting his legs up*
 You must clean here
 here here here
Ferruccio *mops underneath Bruscon's feet*

Scene Three

Half an hour later
Costumes for Nero, Caesar, Churchill, Hitler, Einstein, and Madame
 de Staël on clothes racks
Bruscon *is sitting in an armchair at the back of the hall*
Ferruccio *is erecting a baroque screen on the platform*
Bruscon
 It's the exasperation
 that's important
 it's not our job
 to do people
 favors
 The theater

is not in the business of granting favors
pointing to the screen with his cane
   When Metternich enters
   there's no reason why Lady Churchill
   shouldn't still have her hat on
   it doesn't fall off her head
   until she has sat down
   Sarah has done that quite well before
   But she puts it on again immediately
   Metternich is embarrassed
   because of course he's thinking of Czar Nicholas
   Metternich helps her on with it
   You are always a bit too slow at that point
   on the one hand too slow
   on the other too hasty
   when he's thinking of Czar Nicholas
   and at the same time wanting to do a favor
   for Lady Churchill
   in whom as we know he isn't really interested
   he mustn't bow abruptly do you understand
   After all he is already *Prince* Metternich
   naturally there's still something Coblentzian about him
   The hatpin is lying in front of the screen
   about there
points with his cane
Ferruccio *moving the screen*
inquiringly
   Here
Bruscon
   About there
brandishing his cane
   There
   there
   Of course we mustn't
   leave anything to intuition
   We've planned everything to the last detail
   yet every time we have to start from scratch
   there
Ferruccio *inquiringly*
   Here
Bruscon
   Yes there
Ferruccio *puts the screen down*

Bruscon
He acts as though
he didn't know
where the hatpin is lying
everybody in the world can see
where the hatpin is lying
but he doesn't see it
pretends to Lady Churchill
that he doesn't see it
of course Metternich is already thinking
about Einstein's entry
I know
that's another way I could have ruined my comedy
having Einstein enter
at just this moment
In Gaspoltshofen I deliberately
cut Einstein
whilst banking everything on Madame Curie
pointing with his cane to a spot on the platform
Metternich doesn't know
where the hatpin is lying
he is afraid of Einstein in a way
the Czar has informed him
about a certain Dordiyayev's contrivance
but he cleverly ignores it
The moment Lady Churchill
bends down
I start to dim the lights
Green light on Metternich
while I am already in the process
of making myself into Napoleon
Over there
Ferruccio *inquiringly*
Where
Bruscon
Over there
put the screen over there
Ferruccio *moves the screen to the place where Bruscon wants it*
Bruscon
We ought to have spiked it
with chalk
But of course we don't have chalk any more
there isn't even any chalk
in these provincial holes

Anyway I dim the light
when you are both on the ground
Ferruccio *moves the screen to the right*
Bruscon
That's too far
We don't gain anything that way
that way Lady Churchill's features
appear too pale
pointing with his cane
The screen must come back
Ferruccio *does as Bruscon says*
Bruscon
Stop stop stop
Ferruccio fetches a hammer and nails and nails the screen to the floor
Bruscon
That's good
Metternich is much freer in his movements that way
sudden crescendo of pig's grunting from the surrounding sties
Bruscon *pressing his handkerchief to his nose and trying to stop up his*
ears at the same time—after a pause
Metternich's diction
is not hurried
it's more stately
and of course—in view of the fact
that Lady Churchill knows that the Czar
has sent this dispatch to Napoleon—
his disposition is downright ideal
after a pause
At first I thought
of having your mother play Madame Curie
but that didn't work
To be sure Sarah is not ideal for the part either
in a certain way
everything is a matter of compromise
even when we have our eye
on absolute perfection
everything is matter of compromise
intrigue you know
nothing but intrigue
Humanity caught in a trap
Could you do me the favor
of saying aloud
this sentence
in which Napoleon's character

is most clearly seen
I think that's absolutely necessary Ferruccio
Ferruccio *goes to the edge of the podium*
Bruscon
It's a trifle for you
it will set my mind at rest
to hear this sentence
sound of pigs grunting
Ah well in the final analysis
everything is a matter of compromise
Ferruccio *inquiringly*
Standing
Bruscon
No sitting
sitting of course
Ferruccio *fetches an armchair and sits down*
It is the what has been
the continuing what has been
from there on
please now
Ferruccio
We certainly did not negotiate
without these documents
Bruscon *barking at Ferruccio*
No no
I said from the what has been the continuing what has been onwar
Ferruccio
The continuing the what has been
Bruscon
The other way round Ferruccio the other way round
sound of pigs grunting
Ferruccio
The what has been the continuing what has been
Bruscon
Idiot
I said from there on didn't I
Ferruccio
From there on
Bruscon
From there on
Ferruccio
All right from there on
Bruscon
With head held high naturally

Ferruccio
   With head held high naturally
Bruscon
   For God's sake that's not in my comedy
   I just told you
   didn't I
   It is autumn Ferruccio
   don't forget
   harvest time
   the pigs have stopped grunting
   on the other hand the audience must not notice that
   At least not in Madrid
   where the scene is set
   opening of the Prado you understand
   Retiro Park Variations in the background
   pockets his handkerchief
   You have to know that on the one hand
   and totally ignore it on the other
   do you understand
   what I mean
   England is still completely untouched
   by the catastrophe
   but that's just it
   Your experience comes so to speak
   from Germany
   taking his handkerchief out of his coat pocket again
   Just think of Schopenhauer's *Parerga*
   Nietzsche effect
   blowing his nose
   that's what I intended
   by having Lady Churchill
   lose her hat at the very moment
   that Metternich enters
   pocketing his handkerchief again
   Is everything clear
   Well now
Ferruccio
   It is the what has been
   the continuing what has been
Bruscon
   You must say that with much more meaning
   as if you were saying
   the Pope is coming to tea at four o'clock
   do you understand

as if the Pope
had announced his visit at short notice
all right
Ferruccio
It is the what has been
Bruscon *demonstrating*
It is the what has been
the continuing what has been
Ferruccio
It is the what has been
the continuing what has been
Bruscon
No no
The hat pin has already fallen you see
when you say that
I don't mean the hatpin
I mean the hat
the hat has already fallen
Metternich has already sat down
he is already seated
then he says
it is the what has been
the continuing what has been
Ferruccio
It is the what has been
the continuing what has been
Bruscon
That is precisely what you should have read Spinoza for
you have not read one word of his
it is embarrassing for me
to have to observe that every time
You would have saved yourself and me
a lot of annoyance
if you had read Spinoza
then we could now dispense
with this pedestrian discussion
All right the what has been
Ferruccio
It is the what has been
Bruscon
No no
never mind
It'll come to nothing
rather it will make everything worse

perhaps it's all overrehearsed as well
on the other hand we cannot allow
things to go to rack and ruin
Last night I ran through
the salutation scene once more
with your mother
no improvement there either
this sultry weather
is no good for acting
after a distant sound of thunder has been heard
There's the thunder already can you hear it
At least it will cool things off
a thunderstorm
getting up and going to Ferruccio
The salutation scene proceeds from
the thought about Spinoza
that's a Schopenhauerian trick
I might almost say a Brusconian trick
Sometimes I think
I am Schopenhauer
Bruscon is Schopenhauer
Schopenhauer is Bruscon
Metempsychosis
spiritual homosexuality I think
standing near the platform
Naturally the hatpin comes loose first
then the hat falls off
first of course the loosening of the hatpin
then the falling off of the hat
If you please
do it all again
Ferruccio *has stood up and sits down again*
It is the what has been
the continuing what has been
Bruscon *silencing him with a gesture*
I don't like any of it
What if
we left those two sentences out altogether
Then you would simply say
Listen Metternich
the danger is over
That's better
substantial improvement Ferruccio
Now

Ferruccio
The what has been
Bruscon *striking the air with his cane*
For God's sake
leave it out I said
Ferruccio
Leave it out
Bruscon
Leave out the what has been
Ferruccio
Listen Metternich
the danger is over
Bruscon *relieved*
Excellent
We'll leave out the what has been etcetera
and you start with listen
All right once more
Ferruccio
Listen Metternich
Bruscon *silencing him with a gesture*
That will do
*indicating to Ferruccio that he should make room for him and sitting
    down in the armchair*
The idea was after all
to write a comedy
which encompassed all the other comedies
that had ever been written
Doubtless an absurd idea
But quite within Bruscon's power to accomplish
to himself
worst acoustics imaginable
Here I shall murder
what I have written
with malice aforethought
but my comedy will stand up
even in the most adverse circumstances
to Ferruccio
People will have to hear
what is said
but they mustn't hear too much
the people will have to see
what is shown them
but not see too much
as in all great dramatic literature

the word
is the lifeblood of my comedy
grasps his back while it thunders
After tonight
I shall not be able to move anymore
How healthy I was when we left Gaspoltshofen
as if Utzbach were to be the death of me
Utzbach like Butzbach
If we are bad pupils
we become great masters
that's what your grandfather my father always used to say
on the distaff side naturally
In my *Wheel of History* it is the word that counts
thunder
The reviewers are resorting to
empty-headed watching nowadays
they don't listen any more
Ferruccio *enters with an Empire screen and unfolds it*
Bruscon
We give our all
but it is not understood
the more we beggar ourselves
the greater our mental exertion
the less understanding the criticism
all our lives we perform
and not a soul understands us
Madame Bruscon *as Madame Curie and* **Sarah** *as Lady Churchill*
enter and sit down on armchairs which they have brought with
them
Ferruccio *sits down next to them*
Bruscon *who has not even glanced up*
Lifelong incarceration in the theatre
without the least chance of parole
And yet we never gave up
Penitentiary as theatre
Tens of thousands of inmates
none of whom has a prospect
of parole
The death sentence is their only certainty
thunder
suddenly looking at them all
If only I could draw beer
I thought
white sleeves rolled up

like a landlord
and draw beer
being happy
Really I once wanted to be an innkeeper
bending over and trying the floor of the platform
But I became an actor
went voluntarily to the penitentiary
a life sentence
thunder
getting up as though in pain
Nationally recognized actor
touring company
God
looking round the hall
In one way
I've always hated
the box-seat theatre
the box-seat crowd
turning to his family and shouting
Why are you sitting there
I don't need you
not now
I want to be alone
so be gone
they all rise and exeunt
Bruscon
Talentless brood
thunder
looking pensively at the floor
No question of paying rent for the hall
Paid a hundred and ninety-eight schillings
for the evening meal in Ried im Innkreis
testing the floor of the platform bending over and pressing it with his
hands
thunder
Everything rotten and decayed
As long as we don't fall through here
actually I should demand
danger money
for performing here
getting up again
thunder
When we go on tour
I thought

it will be a process of renewal
for the theatre
so to speak
bending over to the floor and blowing the dust away then getting up
    again
Always did completely
oppositional theatre
looking under the chair into the hall
Actually we are indentured all our lives
to the absurdity
of having been born
Fateful world design
thunder
Error-ridden existence
looking round
cacophonic
idiotistic
sits on the armchair and looking round
Perhaps it isn't all that good
my comedy
world made up of doubt
Landlord *enters at back without Bruscon noticing*
Bruscon *pensively*
Squandered decades perhaps
Sudden loss of hearing I thought this morning
because of the cortisone pills
In the middle of the comedy
my hearing went
but no break in the action
Landlord *approaches Bruscon slowly*
Bruscon *ruminatively*
No rent for the hall
free room and board in Gaspoltshofen
and the doctor treated my ear as well
put distilled Chinese decoctions into it
looks out under the Empire screen
Even if I were completely deaf
I could finish performing
my comedy
thunder
Blindness
that would be bad
deafness only half as bad
Chinese decoctions in my ear

Landlord *has gone to the window*
Bruscon *meditatively*
    Nero Metternich Hitler
    historic constellation
    Churchill the link
    Stockings hand knitted by the landlord's wife
    in Gaspoltshofen
    friendly
    very friendly people
    stroke of luck
Landlord *clears his throat*
Bruscon *as though waking up, sits up straight and says to the landlord*
    Oh so it's *you*
    Sneaking landlord so to speak
thunder
Landlord *advances a few steps toward Bruscon*
Bruscon
    A little attack of weakness
    doubtless
    nothing unusual
    at my age
    Memorizing a few lines etcetera
    Well
Landlord
    The fire chief sends word
    that the emergency exit light can be extinguished
Bruscon
    Can be extinguished
    Yes of course
    It would be absolutely ridiculous
    if the people here in Utzbach
    were to insist upon a restriction
    which no other place has insisted on
    one of the most ridiculous restrictions there could be
thunder
    Of course I thought
    the emergency exit light will be extinguished
Landlord *takes the empty bottles from the table*
Bruscon
    I only drink mineral water
    a man of the spirit
    can do nothing else
Landlord *about to leave*

Bruscon *restraining him*
    In every village I inquire
    whether the cemetery is soggy
    is the cemetery here dry
Landlord
    The cemetery is wet through and through
Bruscon
    Why actually
    in a dry cemetery
    a saturated one is more or less
    ideal
Landlord *exits shaking his head*
Bruscon
    Decomposition conducive
looking around
    It was not my idea to come
    to this Utzbach
    Not under four hundred inhabitants
thunder
    I said
    Agatha's greed
    I sensed it
Madame Bruscon, Sarah, *and* **Ferruccio** *(as Metternich) enter in*
    costume but without makeup and sit down again in their
    armchairs
Bruscon *taking no notice of them, looking at the floor, thunder*
    Perhaps I shall cut
    the third act
    the Churchill scene
    seventeenth scene
    nineteenth scene
    The whole comedy doesn't have to be performed
    in Utzbach
    Before swine
    But the instinct of self-preservation is at stake
    Chinese decoctions
    didn't want to take a fee
thunder
    Signed copy
    of the comedy
    There are still decent people in the country
    Gaspoltshofen was a complete success
thunder

Humanity is still at home in the *Lower* Alps
In the Alps they are all rotten to the core
tourism has destroyed them
looking at his watch
Seven o'clock
Deprived of the tension in the last analysis
No restriction on the emergency exit light any more
turning round and looking at his family
Actors
leading actors
standing and going to the center of the platform
Thought about you
to no avail
No appreciation of art
My fault
My megalomania
My crime
beckoning to Ferruccio to come to him
Ferruccio *steps up to his father*
Bruscon
Just as in Gaspoltshofen
cut the nineteenth scene
seventeenth scene
the Churchill scene
the whole third act
It is time
for you to hang the curtains
Ferruccio *goes and hangs the special curtains at all the windows*
Bruscon *to Madame Bruscon who has been coughing the whole time*
Your hacking will only
delight the hacks
thunder and the sound of rain

Scene Four

Evening
Behind the curtain
Madame Bruscon *as Madame Curie*
Sarah *as Lady Churchill*
Ferruccio *as Metternich*
in costume and makeup seated in armchairs

Bruscon *as Napoleon at the curtain*
peering through a gap in the curtain at the auditorium, very softly
   The house is filling up
thunder and increasing downpour
   Remarkably short people
   remarkably short
   and fat
looking at his actors
   In a certain way
   I have nothing against
   these holes in the wall
   Where there's a will
   there's a way
looking at his shoes and beckoning to Sarah
   Come come quick
Sarah *goes to Bruscon*
Bruscon
   You haven't polished my shoes
   give them a rub
   quickly
thunder
Bruscon *peers through the gap in the curtain while* **Sarah** *polishes his*
   shoes
Madame Bruscon *rises stretches her arms up as far as possible, then*
   bends over as far as possible, far enough to brush the floor, clears
   her throat several times and sits down again
Ferruccio *shakes his head*
Bruscon *to himself*
   Don't turn tail
looking up at the ceiling of the hall
   Never turn tail
thunder
pulling his right foot back
to Sarah
   But you're hurting me
   polish
   not crush
to himself
   Desolation
thunder
   For my part I'm not really averse
   to these desolate places
   yes I often say to myself
looking at his actors

the more desolate
the better
It doesn't matter where you look
no prospects
Sarah *has stopped polishing Bruscon's shoes and sits down in her*
armchair
Bruscon *after peering through the gap in the curtain*
Only because we believe in ourselves
do we manage to endure it
do we survive
thunder
what we cannot change
because we believe in our art
stepping in front of his actors
If we did not have that faith
and even if it's only in the art of acting
we should have long since been in the cemetery
thunder
Nothing interests us
but our art
nothing more
going to the curtain
peering through
looking at the actors
Possessed with tomfoolery
shameless in a certain sense
Stop at nothing of course
thunder
Ne'er-do-wells in a certain sense
incorrigible
peering through the curtain and then looking at his actors again
In this way we escape from
the tawdriness
of national theatres
to himself
Never play in a national theatre again
How I hate the words box seat
thunder
peering through the curtain
About two hundred can stand here
at the back of the house alone
Eight hundred and thirty in the audience
in Gaspoltshofen

But we know that Utzbach has
only just over two hundred inhabitants
My comedy is written so that
even the very last person in the very last row
can catch everything
my comedy is high art
no arcane nonsense
in a certain way I am
a fanatic for the truth
going to the actors
standing in front of Madame Bruscon who has been clearing her throat
the whole time
Madame Curie
was a Pole
don't forget that
I don't care for the Polish people
thunder
not unconditionally
attention-getters
bigotry
the Catholic sort
insipid
but I have always loved
Madame Curie
you don't play her
as someone that I could love
but I'm not going to let you alienate me
from Madame Curie
historic figure
absolutely magnificent historic figure
directly to Madame Bruscon
Careless makeup
Madame Curie especially
can take a lot of black eye shadow
indicating to Sarah that she should bring him the makeup box
All right what are you waiting for bring me
the makeup box
thunder
Sarah *fetches the makeup box and* **Bruscon** *puts more black makeup*
on Madame Bruscon's face
Bruscon
More black round the eyes
I know you like to avoid black makeup

It's revolting
to have to add black makeup
to your face every time
Madame Bruscon *coughs*
Bruscon
That cough
imaginary
hypochondriacal
making up her face for her to the point where it is almost entirely
black
thunder
Atomic age my dear
the whole atomic age
must be in this face
terrible thunder
More or less
the end of the world
in your face
making up her face so that it is finally completely black
Madame Curie
must have a completely black face
is what I've always said
I can't understand
why you don't do as I tell you
Madame Bruscon *coughs*
Bruscon
You spend too much time in bed
We've hardly arrived
before you crawl into bed
while I have to do
all the work
Unhappy disposition
wife
Your hair is
much too loose
taking a comb from Sarah
Combed back severely
I've told you repeatedly
you leave it disheveled
combed back quite severely
à la polonaise
Polish women have their hair combed back quite severely
all Polish women severely combed

combs her hair until it is quite straight
    Madame Curie was ugly
thunder
    I know
    you would like to cut a beautiful figure
    on the stage
    but then you mustn't play Madame Curie
    I don't have a Madame Pompadour
    in my play
    There is no courtesan in my play
    After all it isn't a lewd play
    it is a classical one
tugging at her costume, adjusting her sleeves
stepping back a pace
    If I could only breathe some
    life into you
    but it's no good you're just as stiff
    as when I first met you
thunder
    I could break the spell
    I thought
    breathe life into you
    What a mistake
taking another step back
    But Madame Curie
    was also a stiff person
    an eccentric Polish woman
    stiff through and through
    in the final analysis just as uninspired as you
    that's the truth
    boring in the extreme
    as history shows
    in a certain sense unappealing
    and Polish through and through
    Only she split the atom
    and you only exasperate us
    with your cough
going to the curtain and peering through
thunder
    His Honor the mayor is already there
    A school group curiously enough
turning round to his actors
    A school group

peering through the curtain
    Half price
    but at any rate they're interested
    there *is* certainly interest
    In Gaspoltshofen
    they had a hundred posters printed
    here there aren't even thirty handwritten ones
    clumsy lettering
    hair-raising copy
to his actors
    Bruscon is my name
    I said to the landlord
    not Buscon
    as it is on the posters
    and *The Wheel of History*
    is spelt with a "wh"
    not just a "w"
peering through the curtain
    But I'd be telling a lie
thunder
    if I were to maintain
    that in Gaspoltshofen
    they understood my comedy
    The people were not restrained
    in their applause
    Still this all-pervasive
    stench of pigsties
    Strangely misshapen people
    Most interesting forms of deformation
to his actors
    A paralytic
    in a paralytic's conveyance
    remarkable
peering through the curtain
thunder
    We cannot turn back
    the wheel of history
    that's what I said to the mayor
    A historical diatribe that's what my comedy is
    I said to the mayor
thunder
    Revolutionary
    in a certain sense

master punster
who doesn't despise
a cheap joke either
to his actors
    The house is filling up
    Probably theatregoers
    from the surrounding areas too
    Certainly looks like it
    Hungry for edification
    People striving for culture
going to the actors
stopping in front of Ferruccio
    More of a caricature
    of Metternich
    bad makeup job
    extraordinarily bad posture
    I could almost say
    looks like Metternich
    really a resemblance
    to Metternich
beckons to Sarah to come over with the makeup box
Sarah *steps over to him*
Bruscon *making up Ferruccio*
    Not such a slack face
    at odds with Metternich's spirit
    Metternich is the greatest
    underestimated like no one else
thunder
    and hated
    Elegant bearing
    Elegance after all does not detract
    from intelligence
    that would be absurd
    elegance quite on the contrary
    underscores intelligence
    quite the contrary
    underscores it
    Intelligence is elegance
    indeed
tugging at Ferruccio's costume
    A small supper I think
    light fare
    in this sultry weather

thunder
    It would have been sheer lunacy
    here in in in
Ferruccio
    in Utzbach
Bruscon
    Here in Utzbach
    to play Mozart
    between acts
    Verdi will do just as well
    just as well Verdi will do
    Italianità
    Italianità
tightening Ferruccio's shoelaces and getting up again
    As if this were to be the death of me
going to the curtain and peering through
thunder
    Butchers have quite a beautiful relationship
    to dramatic art
turning to his actors
    Since in Gaspoltshofen
    I ate duck
    today I feel like
    a nice piece of stuffed roast veal
    The best actors
    have to eat meat every day
    Vegetarianism
    does not agree with
    the art of acting
directly to Madame Bruscon
    You are the only one who thinks
    it's possible to survive
    in the long run
    on vegetables
    and those ghastly salads
    Look at you
    A disgrace to the theatre
    a disgrace to the feminine gender
Madame Bruscon *dismisses him silently with her*
    right hand
Bruscon
    Bricklayer's daughter
    My proletarian
    my favorite proletarian

Madame Bruscon *can restrain herself no longer and suddenly bursts*
out into loud laughter
Bruscon *hissing at her*
beside himself
    How dare you
to Sarah
    Sarah my child
    our mother is a mad woman
tremendous thunder
peering through the curtain
    The hall is filling up
looking at his watch
    Twenty past seven
    Almost a hundred people
    But it is a fact that
    almost all my life I have suffered
    from having to be an actor
    If we don't indulge ourselves
    we get nowhere
    possibly
thunder
    I am a megalomaniac
turning to his actors
    like my play
peering through the curtain
    or perhaps not
    But when people
    understand my comedy
    then I don't feel like
    performing it any more
thunder
    The advantage we have
    is that we accuse no one
    only ourselves
    lifelong need for self-accusation
turning to his actors
    Shakespeare
    Goethe
    Bruscon
    that's the truth
as though shaken by a chill
    Fear of freezing to death
peering through the gap in the curtain
    Creature comforts have always been odious to us

roll of thunder
   We preach
   and they don't comprehend
beckoning to Sarah to come to him
Sarah *goes to Bruscon*
both peer through the gap in the curtain
Bruscon
   Philosophical
   through and through my child
dreadful rolls of thunder which refuse to stop. **Bruscon** *and* **Sarah** *look*
      at **Madame Bruscon** *and* **Ferruccio** *who have jumped up in fright.*
Bruscon *staring at the ceiling through which it has already begun to*
      rain while loud cries are heard in the hall
   The parsonage is on fire
   the parsonage is on fire
   on fire
   the parsonage is on fire
the whole audience rushes out
Bruscon *and* **Sarah** *peer through the curtain until the hall is empty*
Bruscon *after a pause*
   The hall is empty
   an empty hall
   perfectly empty
rain drips on them all
Sarah *embracing her father, kissing him on the forehead, very tenderl*
   My dear father
brings him an armchair into which he collapses
Bruscon *after a pause in which the thunder and rain have reached th*
      highest pitch of ferocity
   I might have known that it would come to this

CURTAIN